The Lord Is Our Light

Advent

Scriptures for the Church Seasons

Advent 2017

The Lord Is Our Light

A. ELAINE BROWN CRAWFORD

An Advent Study Based on the Revised Common Lectionary

Abingdon Press / Nashville

THE LORD IS OUR LIGHT
by A. Elaine Brown Crawford

An Advent Study Based on the Revised Common Lectionary

Copyright © 2017 by Abingdon Press

ISBN-13: 9781501847875

17 18 19 20 21 22 23 24 25 26—10 9 8 7 6 5 4 3 2 1

Manufactured in the United States of America

Contents

ntroduction

When God called me to go to seminary, I was puzzled and unsure that I was hearing from God. Attending the seminary that God was calling me to meant moving across the country; leaving my adult children and grandchildren; and selling my house, my car, and most of my possessions. As I sat in a worship service begging for God's direction and confirmation, the Spirit softly said to me, "new beginnings, new beginnings." In the context of the worship service, the echo in my spirit seemed misplaced; but I said, "OK, Lord, I hear you." I moved 2,300 miles across the country to go to seminary with a few clothes, two boxes of books, and no place to live. During my first chapel in seminary, the dean preached a powerful, compelling message, and then he announced the theme for the year—"New Beginnings." For me, that theme was the confirmation that I had heard God, that I was in the right place, and that God was with me on this journey. God came afresh and new that day in a way that even as I write this brings tears to my eyes and joy to my heart. I experienced God's love singling me out in the midst of a room full of strangers who would soon become my colleagues and friends. I praised God that I had listened to the Spirit. My journey over the next three years was one of faith and trust and new beginnings illumined by God's presence on the journey.

Advent is the beginning of the Christian year. It is a time of "new beginnings" for us. No matter what the past eleven months have held, Advent beckons us to remember how much God loves us, even in our brokenness. We get to begin again, with God coming in person to see about us. Advent comes from a Latin word, *adventus,* which means coming. We are invited anew to the pageantry and pain of the Christ event. Jesus comes to us during this season in new ways and new situations, but always as our faithful guide. The Baby born King is both Mary's baby and the Word made flesh, the life and light of the world.

Our readings for this Advent season extend a personal invitation to each of us to walk in the light of Jesus' love, joy, and peace. They also invite us to let our light shine, to be a witness to the new beginnings Jesus has orchestrated in our walk with him. As you read each Scripture passage and its accompanying story, find your new beginning with Jesus. Listen for the Spirit's direction for your life. Bask in the light of God's love for you. Ask Jesus to re-light your candle if your light seems dim. Light extinguishes the thickest darkness. Most of all, during this Advent season, yield yourself to God's fresh approach and God's new beginnings in your home, your church, your community, and even at your job. Allow God to illumine your path this Advent season, and in the words of George D. Elderkin:

> We'll walk in the light, beautiful light,
> Come where the dew drops of mercy are bright
> Shine all around us by day and by night,
> Jesus the light of the world.[1]

---

1 See *http://www.hymnary.org/hymn/LUYH2013/100*.

Mindful Waiting

Scriptures for Advent:
The First Week
Isaiah 64:1-9
1 Corinthians 1:3-9
Mark 13:24-37

The Scriptures for the first Sunday of Advent call us to the sobering reality of our fallen humanity and the need for divine intervention for our salvation. In each of our texts, we find the reminder to examine ourselves, our behavior, and our attentiveness to the things of God. In the Isaiah Scripture, Israel laments over the distance their transgressions have put them from God. They long to recapture their former status and relationship with God. Israel pleads to be remade, reshaped, and remolded by the hands of God. How often have we had to say, "I'm sorry. Please forgive me" to our spouses, our children, our friends, ourselves, and to God? We come to God almost daily asking for a do-over, a chance to set things right and to come back into harmonious relationship with our Creator and Sustainer.

The blessings extended by Paul to the Corinthian congregation in First Corinthians come in the face of a congregation that has forgotten that their gifts were to be used to edify the body, rather than to glorify themselves. How easy it is to lose our focus during this season and to forget or stray away from the true purpose of the season. We can get lost in the gift giving and receiving and forget the true gift of God that we received so long ago, Jesus Christ, who came as a babe and will come again.

Jesus reminds the disciples in the text from Mark to be mindful of how they wait, to be alert and attentive in preparation for the return of the Master. Advent is the season of reflecting on the "signs" of God's illuminating light on our dark paths so that we find our way back to God's presence.

The Scriptures for today also remind us of the love and grace of God that predate our human existence. God's grace was there making a "way out of no way" for Israel, for the Corinthian congregation, for the disciples, and for us. Advent is a season for new beginnings and fresh perspectives on God invading history on our behalf. During this first week of Advent, God's unfailing love, even in the face of our shortcomings, is a dominant theme as we wait expectantly for the light of Christ to come anew to illumine our way.

BLAME OR BLESSING
ISAIAH 64:1-9

Advent is the season of longing to experience God's presence in new ways. We wait expectantly for God to "tear open the heavens and come down" (verse 1). Yet Isaiah reminds us on this first Sunday of Advent that repentance precedes restoration and renewal. Israel has strayed from its relationship and experience of God. The sanctuary lies in ruin (63:18), and Jerusalem is desolated (64:10b). Israel laments the absence of the past demonstrations of God's power and blessings. Israel goes so far as to say that God's anger at them is the cause of their sin (64:5b)! What a darkness of mind and spirit. They seem to have momentarily forgotten that their disobedience is the catalyst of their distance from God.

Comedian Flip Wilson had a wonderful saying that he used to excuse or justify his often mischievous antics. Rather than admitting his own guilt or his contribution to calamity, Flip would say, "The devil made me do it." Soon, you heard adults jokingly using this phrase to excuse bad behavior. When confronted with their contribution to the situation, they would simply laugh and say, "The devil made me do it." This was a joke of the 1980's, but how often do we say, directly or indirectly, like Israel, God made me do it? When we see our personal failings or situations to be a result of what God withheld from us, took from us, or did not do on our behalf, we are blaming God. Blame and blessings seldom reside in the same space.

The blame game began in the garden of Eden. Adam pointed a finger at God's culpability when Adam said to God—"the woman you gave me." Eve blamed her transgression on the serpent, and the serpent blamed God through a misrepresentation of God's instructions (see Genesis 3). There was plenty of blame to go around! Blame often permeates our behavior today. I recall that as young children my brothers and sisters and I would often push the boundaries of our Mom's kindness. Mom would say, "You can go over to your friend's house, but stay in the yard to play." We would go to their home, but we often ran outside the yard after a ball or to sit on the sidewalk to play jacks. On more than one occasion, our pushing the boundary led to trouble. Like the time my brother ran into the street after a ball and barely escaped the screeching wheels of a car. Or the time we decided the yard was too confining for our baseball game, so we went half a block down the street to the park to play, only to be chased home by a stray dog that was wandering the neighborhood. These childhood antics were lessons in obedience. We learned quickly that Mom set boundaries for our good, and when we transgressed them, we could not blame others. We had to take personal responsibility and ask for forgiveness. We were punished for our actions, but the period of reconnecting with Mom's love was always sweet. Even as children, we knew that in spite of our transgressions, Mom loved us and would forgive us. I realized that she set boundaries for me because she loved me. Even though I was disobedient over and over again, she responded to genuine remorse. Personal responsibility, accountability, and repentance can help us to refocus on God's unfailing love—even when we fail.

Israel's behavior and prayers of repentance remind them that they need God. The absence of God's light in their lives reminds them that they are broken vessels, unclean people, and far from the special relationship they once experienced as God's people. They long for the God who acts on behalf of God's people.

When we "come to ourselves," we realize that even our righteous deeds fall short of God's glory. Our righteousness is like filthy rags. Our deeds often carry us away from God's presence, God's grace, and God's blessings. Yet God desires to bless us. How do we know that? We know because in spite of Israel's repeated disobedience, God blessed them over and over again. We also know that to be true because *we* have sinned over and over again, but God is faithful and just to forgive us and cleanse us of all unrighteousness. What a blessing. God tore open the heavens for us. God came down in the form of love for us. God put on flesh and broke open the darkness of oppression for us. Immanuel dwelt among us to show us righteousness in action so that we might experience the light and blessings of following the Way.

In this season, we are not to wait passively for God's presence and blessing. We are called to the lamenting consciousness that we need the light of God to show us the way. Advent is as much a time of lament and seeking after God as the Lenten season is. During Advent, we are called to begin again—to explore the wonder of God's breaking forth into our lives.

We long for God to gaze on us. We long for God to see us as we are and love us, and God does. We long for God's countenance to shine upon us and illumine the way. We long, during this season, to experience the peace of God—not through gifts or even giving but through the blessing of God's joyful, renewed presence in our lives.

During Advent, we look for the coming of God to us in new ways—not in anger because of our falleness, but in love because of God's grace. We are God's workmanship—clay in the hands of the Master Craftsman. Aren't you glad that God mends us again and again?—us, God's cracked pots. God is ready and willing to reform us, renew us, and refresh us, if we will yield ourselves to God's hands. God molds and shapes us during this Advent season (64:8). Reshaping can be painful, like Israel's lament demonstrates. But the restorative joy of being shaped by God to more fully reflect God's light and love is a blessing. As we seek the blessing of God's presence this Advent season, I am reminded of the words of Henry Van Dyke in the third stanza of Beethoven's hymn, "Joyful, Joyful, We Adore Thee." He wrote:

Thou are giving and forgiving, ever blessing, ever blest,
Well-spring of the joy of living, ocean depth of happy rest![1]

Advent is a reminder that God tears open the heavens and comes to us in new ways.

What blame do you need to release? What blessing do you need to claim?

SERIOUSLY?
1 CORINTHIANS 1:3-9

People often express surprise, doubt, disbelief, and amusement all wrapped up in the one word question—"Seriously?" Often, the word is followed with the additional, immediate question—"Who does that?" One may be led to use these popular expressions as we read Paul's letter to the Corinthian congregation. Paul begins this letter with a grace-filled word of blessing to a congregation in chaos. Eugene Peterson comments that "the people of Corinth had a reputation in the ancient world as an unruly, hard-drinking, sexually promiscuous bunch of people."[2] Did Paul forget to whom he was writing? Did Paul forget about the disruption, gossip, and abuse of gifts that pervaded this community? Did Paul forget about the commotion and confusion this congregation had generated? He greets them with grace, with peace, and with blessings—seriously? In spite of the reason for his writing this letter in the first place, Paul offers thanksgiving and blessing to the Corinthians. He says that because of their faith, they will be found blameless before the Lord—seriously, Paul—who does that?

God responds to us first with grace and blessing. I think it would be helpful to our Christian walk if we would look at our behavior in the light of the gospel, and occasionally say to ourselves—"Seriously, does a Christian do that?" Does a Christian act like that or speak like that? Am I emulating the light and love of Jesus Christ in my home, in the community, and in the church? Or is my conduct dimming and diminishing my witness? For Christians, these are individual and congregational questions. Corinth is a congregation of believers whose individual and collective behavior diminished the power of their gifts.

When I was in middle school, I was a straight A student. I really loved going to school. I was excited by new ideas and new adventures through learning. My teachers loved me too and often gave me special responsibilities. The other kids often called me the "teacher's pet." But in the eighth grade, I decided that I needed to add more adventure into my life. The days had become much too ordinary and unexciting. So I decided that I wanted to hang out with the "cool girls" in my school. These were the girls who talked back to the teachers, went to the movies when they felt like it, didn't do homework, and sometimes even cut class. So in an effort to get in with what I thought was the "in" crowd, I cut school one day with a group of "cool" girls. Of course it was clear that I was not cool. I was afraid. I was crying. My mantra was, "We shouldn't be doing this." I kept up such a commotion that they were happy to send me home to my books and science projects! And to make matters worse, my teachers called my mother because I had never missed class. Needless to say, I got in a lot of trouble when the truth came out that I had cut school to go to the movies with my new "friends."

When I returned to school the following week, my teachers were surprised and disappointed in my behavior. But what impacted me, even to this day, was the chastisement I received from my favorite teacher. This was the teacher who had encouraged me and helped me focus on college preparation. This was the teacher who made me work hard to pull out of me the intellect and gifts buried in my eleven-year-old mind. This was the teacher who allowed me to assist her with collecting papers and preparing for the next school day. When I returned to school, she treated me tenderly all day long. She gave me the same privileges and opportunities she had always afforded me. But just before the close of the school day, she pulled me to the side, made me look into her piercing eyes that were filled with tears, and said to me words that changed my life forever. She said, "Don't you know by now that you are a leader and not a follower? You don't need to misbehave to get attention. Be smart, use your gifts, be the leader God intended you to be, and you'll get all the attention you can handle!"

I was crushed that she had waited until the end of the day to speak to me. Now these words would go home with me. I would have to ponder them at the dinner table. They would haunt me in my bed when I was supposed to be sleeping. I would hear them every time my mother spoke of my punishment! Why couldn't she just have been "mean" to me at the beginning of the day like the other teachers, so I could have shaken it off with their remarks?

My favorite teacher, Ms. Yarbrough, loved me enough to see me in the light of God's grace on my life. She saw my potential. She knew that I had temporarily strayed from the path that she had helped set me on. My mother and the community in which I lived used the colloquial phrase, "She got beside herself." That phrase meant that I had gone too far with my behavior.

It was an expression meaning that I was smart, but immature. I was wise in books, but foolish in life. I had book knowledge, but no common sense. Yet my mother, my community, and my favorite teacher all loved me and did not cast me off because of my transgression. They saw in me God-given abilities and potential. They taught me, through their tough love, that gifts without grace disrupt community.

Paul discerns the gifts and the promise of the Corinthian congregation not through human work or conduct, but through the work of the Holy Spirit and the gifts of God in them. As I read this text, I asked myself if this text of blessing to the wayward Corinthians was an appropriate text for Advent. What are we, as Christians and congregations, to discern from this text? Why would the writers of the lectionary place this text at the beginning of Advent? This text is a wonderfully *appropriate* place to begin the Advent season. It reminds us of the work of God in us and on our behalf. We come to this season made aware that God's unfailing love is not dependent upon our gifts or abilities. Our gifts and abilities come only through the grace of God and are to be used to glorify God and to edify the body of Christ. This text is also a reminder that divisions in the congregation must be handled theologically, not just methodologically. Conflict management, counseling, and outside consultants have their valuable place in congregational conflict resolution. But as Paul points out, the best methodology is theological—an opening of ourselves to the reconciling work of God on our behalf. We are to *discern* God's faithfulness in spite of our failures and inabilities. We are to discern God's loving care of us in the midst of the vicissitudes of life. This word of blessing bids us to come to God in this Advent season just as we are—knowing that God loved us enough to bless us with the hope of the world, Christ Jesus.

This text is also a reminder that Advent begins in the messy, smelly stalls of Bethlehem, rather than the glory or glamour of a palace. The church can be a messy, grimy place at times. But God intervenes; first, to bless us with the gift of God's presence, then to direct, challenge, confront, and encourage us. We are called into fellowship first with God and then with our sisters and brothers; this will produce gifts and works that glorify God and strengthen the body in Christ Jesus.

What are your spiritual gifts? In what ways are you using your spiritual gifts to foster unity in the congregation or community during this Advent season?

"BEGIN WITH THE END IN MIND"
MARK 13:24-37

In the 1990's, Steven Covey published a book on leadership and self-development that remains popular even today. He used a catchy title, *The 7 Habits of Highly Effective People.* In his book, he outlines seven keys to leadership and effective living. His second and probably most often quoted principle is to "begin with the end in mind."[3] Covey was talking about literally visualizing your desired results and then taking the necessary steps to achieve your goal. Covey argued that creation happens in two realms, the mental and the physical realms. First, we create in our minds. We envision what our goal or end result would look like. We see the project finished: the degree in hand, the new church built, the presents wrapped and under the tree, or the standing ovation for yet another Christmas pageant. Then, he says, we are ready to begin to put in place the physical creative process to achieve that end. The physical creation is facilitated because we have spent time imagining the end result, so we are better able to discern step by step the necessary processes to achieve a goal.

I got a firsthand experience with this principle of beginning with the end in mind when I had the blessing of having a house built from the ground up. When I first saw the house, it was only on paper. I looked at the plans, the rooms, and the layout and had to visualize the end product in my mind. As my builder and I discussed the plans, I discovered that I could make some changes. I could move walls, open up areas, and I could have a finished or unfinished basement. I could determine finishes, features, and extras. What I could not change was the foundation of the house. It had already been poured in anticipation of a buyer for this house. So I had tremendous freedom within the boundaries of the foundation set by the builder. I visited the site almost daily to be sure that the contractors understood and brought to fruition my vision for the long-awaited house. I never told them when I was coming. I just showed up to observe the work and the progression of the house. One of the elements that I had ordered was a gas, ventless fireplace. That meant no need for the huge chimney stack, no birds flying down the stack, and no carrying wood or removing ashes for me. One day, as I stopped by for my "inspection," I found the workers beginning to stack bricks and to construct a wood-burning fireplace. I was able to have a conversation with the builder, and he redirected the workers to our original design. It was the "signs" of the brick, the location the workers were focusing on, and the materials laid out, that alerted me that the workers had deviated from my design and were constructing a fireplace "as usual." A wood-burning fireplace was not the end I had in mind! This experience is reminiscent of our spiritual journey. Even with a solid foundation of Jesus Christ, we can deviate from the God designated design for our lives when we do not pay attention—moment by moment, day by day—to the in-breaking of God in our lives. The sense of watching and waiting during Advent beckons us to slow down, do daily self-inspections through prayer and study, and to reconnect with the love of God, self, and others.

In our text today, Jesus is telling us to live with the end in mind. Not just the end of our physical lives, but the end of the age. The parable of the fig tree and Jesus' admonitions regarding being alert are visions of living into the "now" and the "not yet." We must be attentive to how we walk in the Way—right now—to be ready for the not yet, that which is to come. Preparation takes watchfulness and being alert to God's activity, now, in our lives. Jesus is not referring to general watchfulness, but to watching with specificity and alertness regarding what we are waiting for. The *leaves* and the *tender branches* of the fig tree point to the season to come and the anticipated fruit. The *specific work of each slave* in the master's house is to be such that the master will be pleased whenever he returns. In both instances, there is a desired result, a goal anticipated that requires being alert at all times, being attuned to the activity around them.

It is significant that this set of parables regarding the coming of the Son of Man is set right before Mark's description of the plot to kill Jesus and the Passion narratives. In Chapter 13, Jesus is giving us a proleptic vision of his death. Jesus tells the disciples to watch, be vigilant, and stay awake. They are about to experience the unexpected. Jesus had warned them of his impending death and the events that would lead to it. Jesus knows his death is impending—he sees the end—and he is telling the disciples what they need to do now to stay alert and awake to the events that are to come.

As Christians, Advent is exuberant for us because we know the end of the story. Several times in this Advent text Jesus tells us to stay alert! We know that after the Passion, death, and burial of Jesus, Resurrection is coming. During Advent, we look for the signs of Jesus coming afresh in our lives as a reminder that Jesus will come again, just as he promised. I think the point of Jesus' message in Mark is that we attend to the signs of his presence everyday in our lives. We tend to be so busy with the activity of the season, so distracted by the social-political climate, so distracted with the technological "advancements" of smartphones, iPads, and multiple digital devices, that we miss the sign of Christ's presence among us. We tend to be over stimulated but under observant, particularly regarding the things of God.

I invite you during this Advent season to begin with the end in mind. Be alert by slowing down and watching for the signs of new beginnings in your life. Build upon the solid foundation laid by God in the sending of his Son in human form to be the lamp to our feet and the light to our paths.

What are you anticipating and watching for during this Advent? How would you like to deepen your relationship with God during this season? What are the signs of Jesus' presence fresh and new in your life? How can you demonstrate your faithfulness as a servant of God by caring for God's house, your body, your community, your church, your family, and your finances?

1. From "Joyful, Joyful, We Adore Thee," *The United Methodist Hymnal* (Copyright © 1989 by The United Methodist Publishing House); 89.
2. From "Introduction to 1 Corinthians," *The Message Bible,* by Eugene Peterson (Navpress, 2002); page 2064.
3. From *The 7 Habits of Highly Effective People,* by Stephen Covey (Free Press, Simon and Schuster, 1989); page 95.

xpectant Preparation

Scriptures for Advent:
The Second Week
Isaiah 40:1-11
2 Peter 3:8-15a
Mark 1:1-8

Advent is a season of expectant preparation. Children are on their best behavior in anticipation of gifts on Christmas morning. Sales clerks are extra friendly, painstakingly helpful, and ready to offer assistance as we are involved in material preparation for the season. The biggest shopping day of the year is usually the Friday after Thanksgiving, when many people are snatching up bargains for Christmas morning. Even our churches spend weeks preparing Chrismon trees, children's Christmas plays, Christmas concerts, and special outreach efforts to the needy. The Scriptures remind us not to be "weary in well doing: for in due season we shall reap, if we faint not" (Galatians 6:9, KJV). Yet we prepare so fitfully that often by the time Christmas arrives, we are exhausted from weeks of preparation and disappointed that the day is "over" in a matter of hours. However, our spiritual preparation during this season is not always as intentional or as rigorous. Our Scriptures for this second Sunday of Advent focus on living in expectant hope while we faithfully prepare for God's fresh in-breaking into our lives.

Isaiah 40:1-11 offers a word of comforting hope in the midst of waiting to the people of Jerusalem: "The LORD's glory will appear" (verse 5). As we read these ancient words, we are reassured that God's tender care takes precedence over our fallen condition. God's love assures us that the valleys of pain will be lifted and the mountains of distress flattened by the glory of the Lord revealed in Christ Jesus. Our hope is an ultimate and penultimate hope. It is based on what God has already done in our lives through the birth of Jesus, and yet, it is also future-directed to the One who will come again. We are to focus not only on failures of the past but also on promises of the future.

We are to be at peace as we wait for the long-expected One. God's delay in no way indicates that God has forgotten God's people. Rather, the writer of 2 Peter 3:8-15 suggests that we keep on living—in holiness and godliness. We are to strive to be more and more Christ-like in our lives. God's slowness is an indication of how patient God is with us. God wants every human to have the opportunity to repent, come to Christ, and choose salvation. So God has not forgotten the promise to return again for the church, but wants as many to choose life as possible.

Mark introduces us to a somewhat strange figure in camelhair who eats locusts and honey, John the Baptizer. It is through this unorthodox vehicle that God beckons us to prepare for the powerful, promised Messiah. The Markan writer skillfully weaves prophesies of the past, John the Baptizer's purpose, and the future coming of a baptism not only with water but also with the power of the Holy Spirit. The Scriptures for today point us toward hopeful expectation as we prepare for the coming of the Savior.

HOPE IN THE HOLLER
ISAIAH 40:1-11

During the funeral service of the civil rights icon Mrs. Evelyn Lowery, Bishop Woodie White preached a brilliantly crafted sermon. He used the topic "Leaving or Going." He elucidated for the mourning throngs of people present the emotional, spiritual, and theological juxtaposition of *leaving* versus *going*. Bishop White talked about *leaving* in terms of departing. He illustrated the pain of leaving with the sadness parents might feel as they prepare for a child leaving home to go to college, the anxiety one might experience in leaving one job to take on a new endeavor, or the pain of losing someone so dearly loved with the throat tightening words—"she has left us." Leaving focuses us on the person or the place that will no longer be a part of our immediate context, whose immediate access we are no longer privy to. Leaving often evokes a sadness or sense of loss on our part. Then he juxtaposed *leaving* with the theological implications of *going*. Going, he said, points to a destination. Going is a word of hope. When a parent's language changes from "my child is leaving home" to "my son is going to Morehouse," or "my daughter is going to Spelman" (or some other great institution), there is a change in the tenor of the voice to one of expectation and promise, even though the pain of leaving is still present. Likewise, the pain and hopelessness of the death of a loved one is softened by the knowledge that, yes, my dearest has left us, but my loved one is going to be with the Lord. The sense of destination elicits hope and comfort. His point, and the theme of our text, is that God's Word offers us hope, even in the midst of difficult situations. The grass withers, and flowers fade, but the hope and strength of God's Word stand forever.

In my book *Hope in the Holler: A Womanist Theology of Hope*,[1] I discuss the resilient hope of African American slave women to persist in the midst of abuse and oppression. Their holler was a primal cry to God to come see about them. The holler was an appeal to God to comfort them in the midst of their suffering and to provide solace in the darkness of spiritual and physical exile. The hope deposited in the narratives of these slave women was a hope based on their trust in a faithful God who would see them through. It was a radical, incarnational hope given by God. Their hope was a bridge between oppression and liberation. The hope of Isaiah functions similarly. It begins in the midst of Israel's holler as indicated in verse one. There is no need to cry "comfort, comfort my people!" if Jerusalem is not upset or in distress and in need of comforting. So it is imperative that we remember the context of this word of hope. The people of Jerusalem have been in exile and have experienced Babylonian captivity, economic devastation, and upheaval of life as they knew it. The prophet is challenging them to cease their focus on what they have left and to rejoice about where God has promised to take them. They are to imagine cities rebuilt, restoration of the nation, thriving economic life, and their restored relationship with God. God offers them a word of hope not based on their current condition, but based on their future, directed with promise and abundant life. It is not based on leaving, but rather, based on where they are going.

Advent is an opportunity to shift our focus to the promised help from God. This season, strangely enough, has one of the highest suicide rates of the year. Why? Because it is so easy to get stuck in the holler of life, the pain, the struggles, what we don't have or can't afford to do—rather than to focus on the hope provided to us in the birth of Christ Jesus. Our hope is based on the knowledge that our joy comes from God *leaving* heaven, giving up the crown of glory to come to earth. When God asked, "Who will *go* for us? God decided to take on flesh, come in person, and dwell among humans to light the way for us. God's destination was not just to come as a baby in a stable. Even in leaving glory, God had a final destination in mind—the Cross and Resurrection. So on this side of Calvary, we can celebrate the birth of Christ preparing the way for us. We understand that the birth of this Child points to a destination for our salvation.

Isaiah also reminds us that we are to prepare for the coming of the Lord. I wonder how much we as a church and society prepare for Jesus afresh and anew in our lives during this season. Certainly, we do gifts, physical preparations for Christmas of decorating trees, who do endless shopping, and multiple parties. But those activities have nothing with preparing for the light of Christ in new ways in our lives. The required is spiritual, internal work aided by the power of the Holy Spirit to enable us to find restoration from our personal and communal exiles. God does not say that we will not have valleys, mountains, and crooked places in life. Adversity, pain, and trial are a part of life's journey. Yet even in the midst of traversing life's difficulties, God claims us as God's own. God cries "comfort, comfort *my* people!" Jesus Christ, the Word made flesh, is the light that makes the crooked paths straight and lifts the valleys of oppression from our lives. Jesus is the light sent from God to illumine our paths back to right relationships with God. He destroys the mountains of depression, anxiety, and stress from our lives—in God's time and in God's way. Advent is a reminder that Jesus Christ is our hope in the midst of the hollers of life.

What do you need to leave behind this Advent season? What holler can you renounce, and what hope do you hold on to? In what ways are you preparing for the Lord this Advent season?

DELAY DOES NOT MEAN DENIAL
2 PETER 3:8-15a

The theme of 2 Peter 3:8-15a is all too familiar to any parent who has traveled with small children for more than an hour. Even if the destination is the child's favorite place, like grandma's house, the zoo, or a long awaited vacation, you have no doubt heard the words—"are we there yet?" The expectation of imminent arrival outweighs any sense of the time, distance, or events necessary to reach the destination. Time seems to stand still for the parent and the child as the words repeatedly fracture the air—"Are we there yet?" "When will we get there?" "How much longer will it be?" Time, for a child, is measured in number of video games played, number of movies played, or number of fights refereed by parents. My brother Steven used to really irritate my mother on our family trips in the car. He would cross his arms, poke out his lips, and offer the constant retort—"we are never going to get there!"

As telling as this may seem, many twenty-first-century adults do not wait impatiently. We live in an instant society. All it takes for most of us to become impatient is a slow checkout line at the grocery, a delay at the doctor's office, traffic at the fast-food window, or a traffic accident slowing all lanes of traffic. We do not wait well because we live in a fast-paced culture and instant microwavable meals, instant credit—which leads to instant debt—rather than talk with others on Facebook and Twitter. We text each other rather cell phone than in person. Road rage is rampant due to impatience. We have instant computers, DSL, and 4G everything to facilitate instant communication. We e-mail greeting cards to each other and Skype a visit with a person who lives across town. Millions of us tweet the details of our lives. The church, too, has become impatient, impetuous, and impulsive. We want drive-by prayers, fifteen-minute Bible studies, and ten-minute sermons. We pray for drive-through breakthrough. We have taken "tarrying" out of our theological vocabulary. We ask people how they are doing, and God forbid if they say anything other than fine. We don't take time to listen to any other response. If we are honest with ourselves most of us, even as adults, don't wait well!

The first-century, Gentile Christians must have experienced the same frustration. They were disappointed because the *Parousia*, the second coming of the Lord, had not occurred. The first generation of Christians, for the most part, had passed off the scene. Had not it been said that the Lord's coming would occur before they all tasted death? The beginning of 2 Peter 3 (verses 1-3) notes that scoffers repeatedly questioned the proposed "second coming" of the Lord. They chided the Christians asking, "Where is the promise of his coming?" In other words, they were asking—where is he and when will he get here? Why is this Promised One delayed? They said not only has the Lord not returned as promised but also "nothing has changed —not since the beginning of creation"—he is an impotent God uninvolved in human history! The inference is that not only is your God delayed, your God is dead! What is taking so long? Why isn't he here yet?

Our text reminds us that delay is not denial. God's time is not our time; for "a thousand years are like a single day" to the Lord. Psalm 90:4 says a thousand years are like yesterday to God. We live in *chronos* time—clock-watching time—minutes, hours, days, weeks, months, and years. We say times flies when you are having fun, but it drags on when we are waiting for something. *Chronos* time is linear time determined by flesh. It's a human demarcation that is killing us—particularly Americans.

But then there is another element at work in this text—*kairos* time. *Kairos* is God's appointed time. It's the time of opportunity—unrestricted by the passing of chronological time. We tend to be unconscious or unaware of *kairos* moments and often don't recognize them until they pass. There is often no external indication that a *kairos* moment is coming, no visible signs that God is about to show up. Ask Moses at the Red Sea, the three Hebrew boys in the fiery furnace, David when he faced Goliath, the bent woman, or the woman with the issue of blood. Ask John Wesley, Dr. Martin Luther King Jr., Fannie Lou Hamer, Henrietta Lacks, or Coretta Scott King if they anticipated the *kairos* moments in their lives. In each instance, it seemed that all human resources had been exhausted when God stepped in—at the appointed time—and performed the miraculous on their behalf. *Kairos* moments tend to happen when you least expect them like a thief in the night and often when, as Howard Thurman put it, "your back is against the wall." Yet God operates in *kairos* time, time unimpeded by the temporality of flesh. God knows that we are impatient humans due to our fallen human nature. So, God is not slow (verse 9) regarding the promised return as these Christians and their critics interpret it. God is patiently waiting on us. Nor is God unaffected by events in human history. It is because of human history, our disobedience and sin, that God waits for us to "get it" that we need a savior. God beckons us to repent and accept the greatest gift ever given. God waits lovingly and longingly for us to "change our hearts and our lives" and accept the gift of grace offered to all humanity—the Christ Child, the Word made flesh. God's delay is a demonstration of patience, not a denial of the promise.

So the text is more than a reference to the eschatological second coming of Christ for which we still await. Christ is not here yet in his final glory! Rather, the text asks us a critical question that deserves a thoughtful, serious answer about how we are to engage time right now. It asks, "What sort of people ought you to *be*" (verse 11) while we wait? It does not ask what are we to *do*, or what business we are to engage in. *Being* has to do with daily living and engagement of life. The text gives us the answer regarding our being in saying we are to "live holy and godly lives" as we wait. The new heavens and the new earth will come, but in the meantime how are we to live in hope and the anticipatory grace of God? God's grace helps us day by day to seek to live lives that move us on toward perfection through the process of sanctification. Yet when we stumble and fall, God's grace is there to pick us up and love us along the way. God says to us through this letter that we are to make every effort to be found by him in peace—pure and faultless. So as an act of God's grace, God sent us the model of being and peace. God gifted the world with the seed of promise, the only begotten Son, the Prince of Peace, the *New Being*, the One we are to emulate. God's delay is not denial. It is peace and promise offered to us again and again through the Christ Child, who will come again.

How have you altered your pace during this Christmas season to hear from God? How can you "be," rather than do, to facilitate the peace and presence of God during this season?

PAST, PRESENT, AND FUTURE
MARK 1:1-8

I am from a generation that enjoys printed photographs and family picture albums. It is not unusual during holiday gatherings for us to converge on the family room and bring out the photo albums. We gather as a family and laugh hysterically as we view pictures of family members and friends. We laugh at hairstyles. We make comments about the clothing—wide collars, bell-bottom pants, and headbands. We remark about the aging process and how some family members "aged well" and other did not. The photos also take us back to times and events long forgotten that still warm our hearts and, for the moment, allow us to relive them. We often remark on family resemblances and differences and how some traits seem to pass from generation to generation. Today, in our digital world, photo albums have taken a different form. We store them on our phones, iPads, or electronic frames. And yes, I have a photo gallery on my phone of my family, friends, places I have traveled, and even the adventures of my dog, who is aptly named Princess. Yet I keep one of my favorite photos in a heart-shaped frame on my desk. A part of almost every day is spent at that desk, writing, reading, researching, answering e-mails, shopping, or just "surfing the web." My favorite photo is a picture of four generations of my family. It displays my mother, my daughter, my two granddaughters, and me. My mother is seated in the foreground holding one granddaughter. I am seated beside and turned slightly behind my mother holding the other granddaughter. My daughter is standing behind my mother and me, holding on to both of us. We all have the same smile, the same high check bones, and our heads and eyes are all focused in the same direction. I love this photo because it evokes a sense of continuity and wisdom passed from generation to generation. It recalls for me the things my mother instilled in me, things I have tried to impart to my daughter and that hopefully she will impart to her daughters. The wisdom comes in new forms with each generation, but there is a sense of preparation and expectancy that emanates from that tradition. There is a confidence that past, present, and future, though distinctly different from one another, have a common denominator of good will, harmony, security, and love.

It seems to me that in our Advent Scripture for today from Mark's Gospel, the sense of past and present are woven together in such a way that they point us to the future. The prologue of Mark deviates significantly from the prologues of the other Gospels. Matthew and Luke begin with birth narratives. Matthew focuses on the birth of Jesus the Messiah, the Anointed One. Luke's birth narrative begins with the birth of John the Baptizer as the foreshadower of the Christ Child. The Gospel of John, in a sense, also begins with a birth narrative. John focuses on the birth of Creation and all that exists through the Word made flesh, Jesus Christ, the life and light of the world. Conversely, Mark's Gospel immediately announces that he is taking us to "the beginning of the good news about Jesus Christ, God's Son." For the author of Mark, this means looking back to the prophetic literature regarding the Son of God. Isaiah had prophesied regarding a forerunner who would prepare the way of the Lord (see Isaiah 40:1-3) and offer comfort and hope to the people. John the Baptizer, in Mark's Gospel, is presented as a modern day Elijah (see 2 Kings 1:8) who points to the coming Messiah. The author of Mark artfully weaves together past, present, and future to point, not to John, but to the Promised One who gives life today, Jesus Christ.

John's message to Israel and to us is one of urgent preparation. We are beckoned to make ourselves ready to receive the One worthy of glory and honor. Preparation involves repentance and confession of sins. This text invites us to take a good look in the mirror and to admit the truth about our lives. My mother had a plethora of "wise sayings" that she often shared with us to help guide and direct our lives. One of her favorites was about truth. She would say, "The truth will set you free. It might hurt your feeling first, and then it will set you free." This text asks us to look at ourselves even if what we see bruises our egos, gives us a temporary pause, or even hurts our feelings. I wonder how often we look deeply enough and long enough to see our own shortcomings, our own failures, our own sins that we need to acknowledge and confess. Rather than reading Scripture through our own preconceived theological lenses, Advent calls us to allow Scripture to read us. By this I mean allowing Scripture to correct our understanding of how we engage the world, each other, and our relationship with God. Such deep self-reflection may expose some of the unorthodox (spiritual) clothing we wear, like John's camelhair and leather belt, and lead us to repentance. This repentance and confession is not for the sake of condemnation, but rather for the sake of cleansing. Advent is another opportunity to be washed in the water of God's Word and to remember the waters of our baptism and the cleansing, saving grace of God.

Repentance also suggests that we are willing to make necessary changes in our lives to get in line with God's direction for our lives. John was clear that his message did not point to him, but to One who was coming after him and who was greater than him. He was but a messenger of the good news. John knew he was not the end of the story, and neither are we. Yet John was a significant part of the prophetic history, and so are we. Our history is linked with God's salvation history and with the history of Jesus Christ. Because Jesus came as a babe more than two thousand years ago, possibility and promise are available to all who follow him.

In Jesus we have past, present, and future connected. Jesus came as a babe in a manger, and we celebrate his coming each year. We revisit the prophecies of Israel announcing his birth and impact on the world. We go to the fields and sit with the shepherds to rejoice again at the angelic announcement that the Savior has been born. Our choirs sing wonderful music of the season and recall for the world the peace and promise of the

Baby born King. Yet all of these events point us to the future. Jesus did not remain a babe in a manager, a teenager at the temple, or a political rebel crucified on a cross. John the Baptizer reminds us in our text that Jesus points us also to the coming of the Holy Spirit to comfort and care for us until his return. The joy of the season is that Jesus is alive and will come back again for his church. Our past, our present, and our future are secure in Christ Jesus.

Discuss how the season might be different if you embrace kairos time rather than chronos time. In what way does your activity during this season point to Jesus Christ? We don't speak much about the Holy Spirit during this season. How might we more fully integrate the work of the Spirit in the birth, life, and death of Christ as a central theme of Advent?

1. From *Hope in the Holler: A Womanist Theology of Hope*, by A. Elaine Brown Crawford (Westminster Knox Press, 2002).

Anointed to Serve

The Scriptures for this third Sunday of Advent provide for us the job description, qualifications, dress code, and code of conduct for the "ministerial candidate." Through the priesthood of all believers, we can all claim the anointing, which is available to each of us to serve God's people. At Cascade United Methodist Church in Atlanta, Georgia, where I served, we had the privilege of developing what we called the Ministerial Candidate Program. The program is designed to assist persons in exploring their calling to serve God in deeper, more meaningful ways. Many of the persons who enter the program feel called to ordained ministry, while some feel they are called to more focused lay ministries. The role of the program is to provide resources, community, and conversation during this discernment journey.

The Scriptures for this third Sunday of Advent help us explore our role as believers. We are, in fact, all "ministerial candidates" on the journey of discerning how to serve God more fully day by day. The Scriptures for today bring us joy in knowing that whatever we humbly present to God can be used by God.

The Isaiah text reminds us that God offers a divine exchange for our tears, despair, and loneliness. Through God's Holy Spirit we find joy in God's assurance that the deficits in our lives, whatever they are, can be corrected by divine love.

As we live in the ordinary routines of life, day by day, hour by hour, 1 Thessalonians 5:16-24 admonishes us to remain joyful and to pray. Prayer is the precursor to peace and joy. Prayer makes serving in difficult times not only possible but also purposeful. Like John in John 1, we can gain clarity about who we are and what God has specifically called us to do when we spend time with God in prayer and preparation for our life journey. John is clear about his role and his relationship to the Messiah. The Scriptures for today remind us to assess ourselves and our relationship with Jesus Christ. What is it that we need to give to God so that our joy is restored? The good news is that, like John, our quirkiness can be used for the Kingdom. God has anointed us to serve God and God's people. Advent is our reminder that God brought us out of darkness into the marvelous light of Kingdom living and service.

DIVINE EXCHANGES
ISAIAH 61:1-4, 8-11

The third Sunday of Advent is traditionally the Sunday of joy. Isaiah 61 begins with the declaration that the prophet is indeed bringing good news of joy to Jerusalem, and to us, in what could be seen as a time of despair. The good news is offered to those who find themselves in less than joyful situations: the brokenhearted, the captive, and the oppressed.

At Cascade United Methodist Church, one of the powerful ministries of this season is called "Hope for the Holiday." It is a ministry that remembers that this is a season of sorrow and pain for some people. It provides a time for those who have lost loved ones during the year to gather, share fond memories, and have a meal together. This year, I will attend this ministry event and experience it through a different lens. In September, two persons very dear to me died. The first was a friend who was like a brother. Our families spent many holidays together over the past twenty years. His sisters are my sisters and best friends. I was there when they buried his father, his mother, and a sister a few years apart. He and his family were there for me when I buried my sister and then a few years later, my mother. His unexpected, sudden death shook my whole family. Two weeks later, my brother Stephen died. He had been in remission from cancer and was doing well, but he became ill suddenly, went to the hospital, and never came home. I think that somewhere in the mix of the year most of us have had some challenges personally, professionally, financially, or politically. We are living in a time when many people are suffering from discouragement, depression, and disillusionment. Yet we can experience joy in the midst of the waves of grief and the flood of activity of this season.

One of the challenges of remaining joyful is that we tend to equate "happiness" with joy, but they are two totally different ways of being because they spring from different sources. One comes from the world around us. The other originates directly from the Spirit of the living God. Happiness is conditioned by and often dependent upon what is "happening" to us. If people treat us well, if things are going well in our lives, then we are happy. If our circumstances aren't favorable, then we are unhappy. Joy, on the other hand, throbs throughout Scripture as a profound, compelling quality of life that transcends the events and disasters that may confront

God's people. Joy is a divine dimension of living that is not shackled by circumstances.

In Isaiah 61, the people of Jerusalem are now out of exile but still existing in dire circumstances. They are living under economic oppression and the resurgence of rituals that dishonor their God and demean them as humans. They also face the daily pressures of living in a corrupted society. (Sounds like twenty-first-century America.) Even though Israel is living in less than ideal circumstances, Isaiah 61 is Jerusalem's good news of divine exchanges. It is a promise of redemption and a promise of exaltation of the afflicted. Soon, the shame and sorrow of Jerusalem will be replaced with eternal joy and prosperity.

In verse 3 of our text, the Spirit declares God's promise and provision to Israel and to us. It underscores the divine exchanges in their present, and in the future, with the coming of the Messiah. Isaiah 61:1-2 foreshadows Jesus' proclamation of good news in the synagogue in Luke 4 when he reveals that his birth, life, and death are the fulfillment of this passage. This text reminds us that Christmas is a time of shopping, gifts, and exchanges—not only department store exchanges but also divine exchanges. God will exchange the ashes of our emotional/spiritual residue for beauty. The word here in the text for beauty has to do with external countenances that reflect one's inner state. Beauty is more than skin deep. Beauty exists in the qualities that exalt mind and spirit. The beauty of the season is not in what you have, but in who has you. It is not in what you can buy, but in remembering the price already paid for your salvation. The joy is not in what you are getting, but in the gift God gave us on that first Christmas morn. That was the dawn of divine exchanges. God wrapped God's self in flesh and exchanged glory for a manger. God exchanged divinity for humanity. God exchanged a place of privilege for a period of humiliation.

The ashes of this world do not compare to the beauty of seeing Christ anew in this Advent season. God provided the oil of gladness—Jesus Christ, Immanuel, God with us—that we might experience new life through his presence. God offers those who mourn the garment of praise instead of the spirit of despair. The spirit of despair redirects your focus from the goodness of God to the residues of human existence. You cannot wear the garment of praise and at the same time wear a hat of misery, a shirt of dejection, a jacket of desolation, a belt of hopelessness, or the shoes of depression. So even during Advent, we are to wear the helmet of salvation, the breastplate of righteousness, the belt of truth, feet shod with the preparation of peace, the shield of faith, and the sword of the Spirit. These are our garments of praise.

The garments of praise eradicate that spirit of despair because God inhabits the praises of his people. First Peter 2:9 reminds the early followers of Jesus (and us), "you are a chosen race, a royal priesthood, a holy nation, a people who are God's own possession…so that you may speak of the wonderful acts of the one who called you out of darkness into his amazing light." We can praise God for exchanging our midnights for day, sickness for health, loneliness for community, poverty for wealth, death for life, weeping for joy, enemies for footstools, tests for testimonies, and trials for triumphs. God offers us beauty in exchange for our ashes and oil of gladness for our mourning. God became our garment of praise to destroy the spirit of despair. Joy that lasts is evidenced in the lasting awareness that God is with us. It is grounded in the divine exchanges that bring us out of darkness into God's marvelous, promised light, Christ Jesus.

What attitudes would you like to exchange during this Advent season? In what ways has God brought you out of darkness into the amazing light of the season?

LIVING IN THE LIGHT
I THESSALONIANS 5:16-24

When I enter my house from the garage, the first thing I see is a plaque that I hung on the wall fifteen years ago. I call it my life plaque. It says, "Life is what happens to us while we are making other plans." It reminds me to live each day to the fullest. I placed this plaque at my garage entrance because I use that entrance each day and sometimes more than once during any given day. I use it for the ordinary happenings of life such as bringing in the groceries, taking out the trash, and going in and out to walk my dog, Princess. I enter here when I return home from church contemplating a sermon or a comment made by a parishioner, from making hospital visits to parishioners faced with unexpected illness, and from having "fun time" with my granddaughters. The plaque reminds me to treasure each moment.

The main entrance of my house opens to the living room where colorful, decorative art greets my friends and visitors. While this artwork is often commented on for its beauty, uniqueness, and color, its message is a fleeting impression on its observer. On the other hand, the "life" plaque is rather plain. One really could easily overlook it, and I am sure it will never win a rare art award. But the life plaque is the grist of living. Life happens to us *while*…is a reminder that all we have is right now, today, this moment.

Much of our energy is spent reminiscing or bemoaning the past or planning for the future. But the reality of life is that most of it is lived in what we preachers call "the meantime." The meantime is the in-between spaces of life where we find ourselves most days. It is ordinary time. It is going to work, preparing meals, visiting family or friends, conversations in the grocery store, caring for aging parents, attending school, and taking exams. The list goes on. The meantime is where the substance of life occurs. In many ways, it is the crucible of our faith. Our experiences in everyday living refine and define our faith. The meantime is where God's power and promises coalesce to facilitate human purpose. Hope, joy, possibility, and purpose emerge in the ordinary activities of life. If we do not find ways to enjoy today, regardless of circumstances, then we miss the opportunity to live fully.

First Thessalonians seems to be a litany for living in the "meantime." People in the early church lived in expectation of Christ's imminent return. They were disillusioned and disappointed that the second advent of Christ had not occurred as Jesus and the prophets had prophesied. Paul said in 1 Thessalonians 1–2 that there was no need to second-guess when the day of the Lord will come. It would come when they least expected it, like a thief in the night. In verses 5-6, he said they were children of light and to stay awake, alert to the times and sober minded. Paul reminded them that life goes on and must be lived. As children of light they were to live in a way that pleased God.

Paul said to them, and says to us, get on with living. He elucidates the elements of living in the light of God's Spirit. "Rejoice always" and "pray continually" are tall orders (verses 16-17). Yet joy and prayer are two sides of the same coin. The Greek for "pray continually" means, "pray *without intermission*," without allowing prayerless gaps to intervene between the times of prayer.[1] This does not mean that we are on our knees twenty-four hours a day or that to be truly faithful we need to lead a sequestered life of prayer. But what it does mean is that our lives are to be so drenched in prayer that praying is as regular and as normal as breathing. John Wesley, the founder of Methodism, taught that joy and prayer were directly connected. Wesley remarked that "rejoice evermore" (KJV) means that one is to live

> in uninterrupted happiness in God. Pray without ceasing—Which is the fruit of always rejoicing in the Lord. In everything give thanks —Which is the fruit of both the former. This is Christian perfection. Farther than this we cannot go; and we need not stop short of it. Our Lord has purchased joy, as well as righteousness, for us. It is the very design of the gospel that, being saved from guilt, we should be happy in the love of Christ. Prayer may be said to be the breath of our spiritual life. He that lives cannot possibly cease breathing. So much as we really enjoy of the presence of God, so much prayer and praise do we offer up without ceasing; else our rejoicing is but delusion. Thanksgiving is inseparable from true prayer: it is almost essentially connected with it. He that always prays is ever giving praise, whether in ease or pain, both for prosperity and for the greatest adversity. He blesses God for

all things, looks on them as coming from him, and receives them only for his sake; not choosing nor refusing, liking nor disliking, anything, but only as it is agreeable or disagreeable to his perfect will.[2]

Living with joy in the "meantime" means, as Wesley indicated, that we bless God in all things and situations. Living life in the Spirit indicates a conscious awareness of God's presence so that we can "enjoy God's presence" no matter what the circumstance or situation.

Life is what happens to us as we are making other plans. Life in the light of the Spirit is a joyous life. Joy does not mean freedom from trials and tribulation. What it means is that our joy is grounded in the awareness and assurance that the God of peace is always with us. The Spirit illumines our path and leads us through the vicissitudes of life. The joy of this third Sunday of Advent rests in living everyday life in the light of God's Spirit, moment by moment.

How have you discovered the beauty of living each day to the fullest? In this Advent season, how might you experience the light of God's presence more fully? What do you discern the Spirit speaking to you during this season?

WILL THE REAL MESSIAH PLEASE STAND UP?
JOHN 1:6-8, 19-28

My mother rarely watched television. She was always busy cooking, ironing clothes, cleaning the kitchen, doing laundry, or some other needed household task. She seemed to be in perpetual motion. She would hum or sing and seemed to enjoy what I considered to be "chores." She taught children how to read during the day at school, and from the awards and gifts she often brought home, I am sure she was just as happy and productive at work. It was a rare treat for me as a child to have my mother actually sit down to watch television with me.

She did enjoy one show, however, and we would watch it as a family almost every week. The show ran in the early 1960's, and though I really did not understand her fascination with the show, I would watch it with her. It was a game show called *To Tell the Truth*. There were usually three contestants on a panel. One was the central person, while the other two were imposters pretending to be the central character. Each contestant on the panel would be asked a series of questions about their lives and occupations. The questions would be asked by featured celebrities who were playing the game that week. The questions were intended to reveal the true identity of the central contestant of the week and to expose the impostors. The show host would begin the process by asking the contestants to state their names. Each would say, "My name is …" and give the central character's name. So all three contestants would claim to be the central character. Then, through a series of questions, the identity of the true central character would be revealed. What was also interesting about the show was that the real central character could not lie in response to the questions posed to him or her. The impostors, however, could embellish their answers or even lie in response to the question in order to convince the judges that he or she was the central contestant.

As a family, we would listen closely to the answers from each contestant, and then we would have a running debate regarding which one we thought was the true central contestant and why we had selected that person. It seemed to me that we were solving a great mystery novel. After the period of questioning had subsided, the host would ask the question the entire television audience was waiting to hear, "Will the real … please stand up?" There would be a minute of hesitation. Sometimes two people would motion as if they were getting up, but finally the real central contestant would stand up. Quite often we were absolutely shocked with the outcome. We had our own preconceived notions of what that person should be like. We had thoroughly debated which questions had been answered correctly. And, for each of us, our selected contestant had surely been the most convincing. The bonus to the show was that after the central character revealed his or her identity, the other contestants would share their occupations, which were usually as surprising as the occupation of the central contestant. As a family, we would laugh, share surprise, and gloat if we happened to have correctly identified the mystery contestant.

First-century leaders played a similar game by attempting to identify the Messiah. In John 1:19-28, the inquisition of John suggests that they are doing an identity check. "Who are you?" they ask (verse 19). He clears up their query straight away by responding, "I'm not the Christ" (verse 20).

Two thousand years removed from Bethlehem, we also know that we are not the Christ. As Christians, we know the Messiah's incarnational presence is no longer among us, but we also know that he will come again. The looming questions from this Advent text to us are "Who are you?" and "What do you say about yourself?" (verse 22). In what way does your life "testify concerning the light?" (verse 7). John was clear regarding who he was and his mission in relationship to the Messiah. John knew that he was "a voice" (verse 23) preparing, proclaiming, and announcing the coming Messiah, the light. He was sure of his identity and purpose in life. He answered the questions posed to him by the religious leaders with directness and certainty.

In light of Jesus' birth, death, and resurrection we can be certain about who we are. Like John, our identity and purpose in life are directly connected to our relationship with Jesus Christ and his activity through us in community. We are joint heirs with the Baby born King. We are adopted children into the family of God. Jesus Christ, our elder brother and friend, is our Savior. We are children of the light, lead by "the true light" (verse 9). Advent reminds us that we can respond clearly, directly, and with certainty regarding who we are and whose we are. Our identity is made clear in the Word of God.

Part of knowing who we are has to do with knowing who we are not! We are each gifted to serve the body of Christ, but none of us has all the gifts. However, when we each function in our area of giftedness, the body of Christ is able to minister effectively. We should ask God, during this Advent season, to stir up the gifts in us. We are admonished in Matthew 5:16 to let our light shine before people, so they see the good things we do and praise God.

I remember a story that circulated some years ago regarding a child who frequently attended church with his mother. Like most children, he would often become restless during the worship service. He would stand up at inappropriate times, talk a little too loudly about the service, write on the giving envelops, play with his cars, and he just could not seem to sit still for more than a minute or two. He began to stand up several times during the service and his mother made him sit down each time. Finally, exasperated with him, she said to him, "You better sit down and do not get up again or you will be in serious trouble." The child sat down hard on the pew, crossed his arms across his chest and said to the mother, "I might be sitting down on the outside, but I am standing up on the inside!" We can get restless and frustrated with the commercialization of Advent, but I wonder if Jesus Christ stands tall in our lives during this season. I wonder if our identity is clear, based on the evidence of our lives. I wonder if the power and glory of the season shines through our living and our giving. During this Advent season, will the real Messiah, in each of us, please stand!

What is unique about your story? How has God used that uniqueness in the body of Christ? What would it mean to have the real Messiah stand up in your life, church, community, and nation?

1. From *Commentary Critical and Explanatory on the Whole Bible*, by Robert Jamieson, A.R. Fausset, and David Brown, 1871, public domain. *http://www.biblestudytools.com/commentaries/jamieson-fausset-brown/1-thessalonians/1-thessalonians-5.html* (accessed April 17, 2017).
2. From *Wesley's Explanatory Notes*, by John Wesley, 1754 and 1765, public domain. *http://www.biblestudytools.com/commentaries/wesleys-explanatory-notes/1-thessalonians/1-thessalonians-5.html* (accessed April 17, 2017).

Humans Plan, God Laughs

Scriptures for Advent:
The Fourth Week
2 Samuel 7:1-11, 16
Romans 16:25-27
Luke 1:26-38

A Yiddish proverb says, "Man plans and God laughs."[1] The wisdom in this statement is the realization that human plans, as grandiose as they can be, are often shortsighted. Our human perspective is so limited, but God sees the end from the beginning. God admonishes us not to lean on our own intelligence, but to allow God to direct us on a straight path (Proverbs 3:5-6). We make so many detours in life simply because we think we have things figured out. We think that we know the way to go or what to do. In actuality, our vision is limited, and our perspective is skewed. God has plans for us that will prosper and benefit us.

In Second Samuel, David brings what he believes to be a plan that will honor God. The amusement in his plan is that because he has a beautiful home in which to dwell, he plans to build God a house in which to dwell! So often we want to box God in based on our limited human perception. So God redirects, delays, and sometimes vetoes our plans in order to bless us. Usually when we look back, we see how the detours were for our development.

Paul reminds us in Romans 16:25-27 that we are to glorify God for our earthly journey. God sent Jesus, the light of life, into the world that we might have abundant life. Paul says our response, in spite of our human limitations, is to praise and worship our faithful God. Prayer and praise help us to hear from God so that we are open to the leading of the Holy Spirit. The readings for this fourth Sunday of Advent beckon us to surrender our plans to God, the God who loved us so much that he came in person to save us and guide us as we strive to walk in the light.

Mary and Joseph's life took a divine detour when the angel announced to Mary that she would conceive and bear a child by the Holy Spirit (Luke 1:26-38). God had plans for them, plans that seemed scandalous at the time, but they were for their salvation and ours. The unplanned child, born to a virgin, in a stable, would save the world. Humans plan and God laughs! God's ways are not our ways, and God's plans are not our plans.

DIVINE VETOES
2 SAMUEL 7:1-11, 16

As I think about the Yiddish proverb, I wonder if God ever stops laughing given the plans we make and bring to God. I can imagine that tears roll down God's face in amusement at our plans. We tend to plan based on what we want or what we feel is best for our life or situation. My life plan was to become a registered nurse so I could earn a "good living" and help people. I would have job security because "nurses are always needed." My plan was to exercise the freedom of mobility that a nursing degree affords one and travel the world, or at least the country, as a travel nurse. With marriage, three babies, and aging parents, those plans quickly changed. My plan B was to become a nursing administrator managing nurses, working with doctors, and interacting with patients. After years of hard work and focused direction, I achieved that goal and became the administrator of a Same Day Surgery unit. This meant, in addition to great pay, no more working weekends, a steady shift of 9–5 P.M. every day, and the ability to wear street clothes rather than uniforms! Throughout the journey to my goal, God was calling me to ministry. My plan for ministry was to serve God, and people, by being a nurse administrator. After all, staff often came to me for consultation and personal direction. I often had opportunity and occasion to pray with an anxious patient or to comfort a distraught family member. The bonus was that I was serving God and making a substantial income with great benefits! What could be better than that? But those were *my* plans, *my* career path, and *my* financial strategy. Six months after attaining my career goal, I felt very deeply in my spirit that God was calling me to go to seminary! My response to God was—can't you wait! Let me "do my thing" for a few years, save up enough money to live comfortably, and then go into the ministry? God laughed!

Planning was not the problem. A career path is a noble undertaking, and Scripture reminds us that "the prudent give thought to their steps" (Proverbs 14:15). The problem was, as the poet Robert Burns wrote, "The best-laid plans of mice and men oft go awry."[2] In his poem "To a Mouse," the eighteenth-century poet wrote about a little field mouse who works diligently for a long time building his home in a field only to have it overturned and destroyed in one routine plow by a farmer and his tractor. Burns's point in the poem is applicable to life. His point is that no matter how well we plan,

THE LORD IS OUR LIGHT

no matter how well intended our plans may be, there are often unforeseen circumstances that interrupt or dismantle our best intentions.

It is remarkable that in our text the well-intended plans, of human origin, are not God's plans. King David tells the prophet *his* plans. Nathan affirms David's plans based on *his* assumption that God will be pleased. Neither of them asked *God* what God desired. Our best thinking often crumbles under the weight of divine insight. We cannot anticipate how God will break into human history, into our lives, or into our plans. God often confounds and confronts our limited human expectations. God's plans are not our plans, and God's ways are not our *ways* (Isaiah 55:8). Our hubris lies in planning without consulting God. We often devise our plans and then bring them to God for a blessing, like David. We have to be reminded that God is the divine provider, rather than a celestial recipient of human generosity. As my mother would say, David seems to have momentarily "gotten beside himself." He got "too big for his britches." His focus is on what he will do for God. God reminds David that he has been guiding and caring for him from being a shepherd over sheep to being a king over God's people. God surprises him with, "You are not the one." Too often we think we are the one to advance God's kingdom when we may actually be the one who prepares the way for God's plans to come to fruition. God has plans for David that are greater than anything David can imagine—plans that exceed one house, or one temple, or even one generation. David offers God a destination, a place where God can reside; but God offers David a dynasty, a kingdom that will never end.

What a wonderful Scripture for Advent! This text is a reminder that God may veto the "best laid plans of mice and men"—even of God's chosen servants. God is the author of detours and changed destinations. Divine surprises are one of God's specialties. Christians see the dynasty promised to David fulfilled in a baby, Jesus, Immanuel, God with us. Who would have expected a baby born among animals to a poor couple in an obscure land would be the key to a kingdom that would never end? God laughed as the kings and prophets watched for a political king born in wealth and status, who would overturn the government by force. God vetoed the quiet, unassuming life that Mary and Joseph probably had planned for themselves. God is amused, I am sure, at our plans, not only during Advent with our focus on shopping and parties but also at the plans we have for our lives that fall so short of what God offers us. Advent is a time of wonder, awe, discovery, and surprise by God. It is not a time to give God our wish list. It is a call to open ourselves to hearing and experiencing the Christ in new ways. Advent calls us to remember God's in-breaking into our lives and all that God has already provided for us.

God has veto power over the shortsighted plans we envision for our lives. Divine course corrections have been a part of the journey throughout human history. As I look back over my life, I am so thankful that God vetoed some of my plans and surprised me by leading me in a totally unexpected direction for my blessing. Advent beckons us to risk going to God to seek out God's plans for our lives, to get a fresh perspective on the working of God within us. Advent calls us to remember and celebrate that God surprised us all in the gift of hope born anew, Jesus Christ. Surrender your plans, your calling, and your life to God; and be open to God's vetoes and God's surprises.

What plans has God vetoed in your life during this Advent season? How was your understanding of God at work in your life changed? What plans do you have that need to be taken to God? What has been your response to course corrections?

PRAISE YOUR WAY THROUGH
ROMANS 16:25-27

Romans 16:25-27 is both a doxology and a call to worship. Worship, praise, and blessing are circular events in the life of a Christian. Paul begins in Chapter 1 of Romans with a greeting succinctly recalling the good news through Jesus Christ. Paul shows the connecting thread through the messianic prophecies of the Old Testament, through the lineage of David, to Jesus. This good news was manifested in the flesh in the birth of the Christ Child. He was declared publicly to be the Son of God, endowed with power from on high, who died for our sins and arose from the dead. Jesus Christ, the Son of God and Son of Man, sent the Holy Spirit to indwell Jews and Gentiles so that we might live in the grace and power of the Spirit. Paul connects for us 2,000 years of prophetic history, its fulfillment, and the resulting human blessing; and he does it in six introductory verses of this Letter to the Roman congregations (Romans 1:1-6)! What good news!

Yet, the good news in Jesus Christ is revealed in the light of the human condition. After thoroughly discussing the trials and triumphs of the human condition in Chapters 1–16, Paul concludes this conversation with the Romans with a call to worship the One whose Word never fails. Paul's prayer of blessing comes full circle and reminds us that it is the good news in Jesus Christ that strengthens us. His concluding prayer emphasizes that we are to give glory, praise, and honor to the God who strengthens us. Our strength, he reminds us, lies in the secret that was proclaimed by the prophet Nathan (2 Samuel 7:1-11, 16) and revealed in the announcement to Mary (Luke 1:32-33). The angel told her that the Holy Spirit would come upon her and the one conceived in her womb, the Son of the Most High God, would be given the throne of David. Mary is a part of the connecting thread of grace that links Jesus to the throne of David and humanity to the throne of God.

The *mystery* of God is revealed and made available to all. The rejected are welcomed. The weak are made strong, and the ostracized are included. What good news!

In this Advent season, Paul's text to the Romans pushes us to praise God for all of God's blessing through the secret born in our Savior, Jesus Christ. We are to be a part of the praising community, acknowledging our connection to one another and to God. Paul uses the term glory *(doxa)*, which really means to praise, to honor, and to worship God (verse 27). In our worship, we acknowledge who God is. We celebrate God's majesty and awe. We acknowledge that God is life and light and the source of all that exists. Our worship moves to praise of God's acts on our behalf. We praise God for, as my mother would say, the "activities of our limbs"—even when filled with pain and limitation. We praise God for mercy and grace that we experience, day by day, moment by moment. For without the birth of the Baby born King, none of our praise would be possible. So, in spite of or in light of the human condition, Paul reminds us to praise our way through.

There is a wonderful popular gospel song that emerged in the latter part of 2013 and is being sung by congregations nationally and internationally. The song was written by Hezekiah Walker and is titled "Every Praise."[3] It is a very simple song, but congregations often erupt into spontaneous praise as the words of the song sink deep into their souls. The chorus of the song reminds us all: "Every praise is to our God." This seems to be Paul's message in our Scripture for today. He says our praise, our adoration, our worship, our hallelujahs have their origins in God's in-breaking into the world. The Word made flesh is due our praise. Walker reminds us that God is our Savior, our healer, and our deliverer. That's the mystery of our faith—that the Christ Child, the light and life of the world, saves us, heals us from the power of sin, and delivers us from all forms of oppression. That good news strengthens us to praise our way through difficult situations and offer faithful obedience to our God.

Paul connects faithful obedience with praise (verse 26). Mary and Joseph demonstrated faithful obedience. They trusted God even when they did not fully understand their divine connection in the unfolding of God's plan. They trusted God to direct their path. Our praise can be grounded in that same faith. Jesus came into the world to be a lamp to our feet and a light to our path so that we can faithfully follow him. We gain strength, even in our trials and tribulations, when we obey Jesus and faithfully serve him. Praise focuses us on God rather than our problems or difficulties. Praise also reminds us of just how blessed we are regardless of our circumstances.

The joy of this season is echoed in the words of the hymn "Joyful, Joyful, We Adore Thee."[4] In the hymn, God is called "God of glory, Lord of love." It says that when we praise our God, our hearts open like gentle flowers responding to warm sunshine. God's love illumines our darkest days and replaces our sadness with joy. God is the "giver of immortal gladness" who fills us with the light of love! The source of our joy and strength is in God's greatest act of love, the mystery revealed—Christ Jesus. I invite you to sing the words of this hymn and listen to the gospel song "Every Praise." Or, engage in that act that reminds you of God's presence and God's faithfulness. Then, whatever you face, pleasant or unpleasant, during this season, you have a reminder that God invites us to praise our way through and let the glory of the Lord strengthen us.

What activity or music reminds you to praise God? What does it mean to you when Paul says to give glory to God "who alone is wise"(verse 27)? How do the words to "Joyful, Joyful, We Adore Thee" and "Every Praise" inspire or challenge you?

SCANDAL
LUKE 1:26-38

The story of the Annunciation is just remarkable. In fact, its details have been debated throughout the centuries. Books have been written, movies made, and rumors circulated regarding Mary and the birth of Jesus. Imagine the shock of having an angel appear to you and declare that the Lord favors you and is with you! This in itself makes this story hard for many to believe. Angels didn't just appear to anyone, especially to a woman, in this time and Jewish culture. Mary was not a wealthy woman nor was she an influential person. Why had God chosen her? The angel tells her that she is so favored that she, an unmarried, teenage virgin, is going to have a baby! Scandalous! Now this is not going to be just any baby. This child is going to be the Messiah, the Son of the Most High. I am sure by this point Mary is so overwhelmed that she is not sure what to make of this information. Mary knew about the prophesied Messiah, but I am sure she was shocked and surprised that God would come to her, in her situation, in that place, at that time. In the vernacular of the ABC television show *Scandal*—"Somebody call Olivia Pope because Mary needs 'a fixer'!" The fixer surprises everyone with unique solutions to any situation.

We have the privilege of looking down the road into Mary's life to see what this scandalous "favor" affords her. Ultimately, she would bear the Christ Child. What an honor to be invited to be *theotokos*—the God bearer. What an honor to be an instrument of the incarnational coming of God to fallen humanity. But being favored by God also meant that Mary—a poor, young, and unmarried girl—was asked to be (in our vernacular) a teenage, unwed mother. This "favor" could spoil her intended marriage to Joseph, ruin her reputation, and even worse, get her killed. She and Joseph would have to go on a long weary journey to a small town to register, not because they wanted to go, but because they were commanded by Caesar Augustus to enroll in the tax lists (Luke 2:1). When she went into labor during the trip, there was no plush, sterile hospital for her labor. There was no comfortable birthing room and no epidural. There was not even room in the inn for this "favored one" to be afforded privacy in giving birth to the Christ Child. No apparent favor existed in giving birth in a stable among the animals. This favor would also bring her the opportunity to see her beloved son rejected, ridiculed, whipped, spat upon, tried, convicted, and crucified! Scandalous! We tend to think of being favored by God as a life of pleasure, popularity, and prosperity—when it often includes an invitation to suffering and sacrifice and to move beyond always being socially acceptable and politically correct.

Mary's response to the angel's announcement is, "How can this be, since I am a virgin?" (verse 34, NRSV). In other words she said that the task seemed unreachable because of her human limitations. Her question says she has not done what it is necessary to do—in the normal human course of events—to make this request a realizable possibility. How can you do this miraculous thing in me when I've not met the human requirements? How can you do this miraculous thing in me since I am inadequately prepared? "How can this be?" Aren't these the same questions we ask when God wants to do a new thing in us?

The question is not about God's ability; it's about our *inability*. We tend to think of how we haven't met the human requirements that position us for God to do the miraculous in our lives. We say things like: I'm too poor, I'm the wrong gender, I'm the wrong ethnicity, I'm undereducated, I'm over educated, I'm miseducated, I'm too young, I'm too old, I'm inexperienced, I'm over experienced and so forth. The list of deficits goes on. But, like Mary, when the Holy Spirit comes upon you, you will receive power—the power of the Most High overshadows you—that which is conceived in you, that which God allows to be nourished in the womb of your humanity— will be holy. The New Revised Standard Version of the Bible translates the Greek word *episkiazō* as "overshadows" in this text. It is closely associated with the Old Testament idea of a cloud that symbolizes the immediate presence and power of God. When God overshadows you, female or male, God takes possession of your very being. Whether or not you have ever experienced physical pregnancy, God calls and equips us to give birth to the holy in our lives, in a particular time, in a particular location, for the blessing of a particular people.

As scandalous as the Incarnation may appear to be, Advent calls us to consider that nothing is too hard for God. We are challenged to open ourselves to new possibilities in our lives. God does more than break into human history; God imparts and empowers us to walk uncharted paths. We are invited to become willing participants in God's divine disruptions. We become partners with God. Our "fixer" is the Holy Spirit sent from God to our particular condition of existence. Yet just as with Mary, God awaits our response to the divine invitation. Mary's response was "I am the Lord's servant. Let it be with me just as you have said" (verse 38). As theologian Cynthia Rigby notes, Mary becomes "a creative partner and agent with God in the coming of the Christ child."[5] What is our response during this Advent season? Whom do we serve—God or ourselves? The One we serve informs the latter part of our answer. Do we dare respond like Mary, opening ourselves to miraculous intrusions into the ordinariness of our lives? God's greatest gift to us was the incarnational presence of God's Son. Our greatest gift to God is "faithful obedience" (Romans 16:26), like Mary and Joseph. Favor includes risking ourselves to serve a self-giving Savior. The scandal of Advent is that we dare say to God, "I am [your] servant. Let it be with me just as you have said," and mean it.

Has God ever made a scandalous request of your life? What was it? How did you respond? In what ways has Advent been an invitation to cooperate with God's plan for your life?

1. See *http://www.yiddishwit.com/gallery/laugh.html.*
2. See the original poem and an English translation at *http://www.essentiallifeskills.net /toamouse.html,* (accessed April 18 12, 2017).
3. See lyrics at *http://www.azlyrics.com/lyrics/hezekiahwalker/everypraise.html,* (accessed April 18, 2017).
4. From "Joyful, Joyful, We Adore Thee," words Henry Van Dyke and music Ludwig Van Beethoven. *The United Methodist Hymnal;* 89.
5. From *Feasting on the Word: Preaching the Common Lectionary* by Cynthia Rigby, edited by David Bartlett and Barbara Brown Taylor (Westminster John Knox Press, 2008), page 96.

*A*n Word and Song

Scriptures for Advent:
Christmas Day
Isaiah 52:7-10
Hebrews 1:1-4 (5-12)
John 1:1-14

Christmas Day is a time of celebration in word and song. The air is filled with thanksgiving, reflection, miracles, and awe. Today, we are tossed between the cradle in Bethlehem and the crown of glory. Our minds and hearts celebrate the birth of the Christ Child, yet our spirits give thanks for the cross and the resurrection to new life. The music of the season is fulfilled today in the presence of our Savior. Emmanuel has come, we give glory to the newborn King, and we come this day to worship and adore Christ, the Lord. We experience the kin-dom of God, God's tangible fellowship with humanity that brings us into relationship with each other.[1] In the midst of the celebration we remember those who are the least, the lost, the disenfranchised of the world. And we praise God for a Savior who has experienced all the vicissitudes of life.

Our readings for today call us to the somber and the celebratory aspects of Christmas. Isaiah 52:7-10 speaks of the jubilant feet of the messenger, running to announce peace and salvation. They are "happy feet" because of the salvation of the Lord. The prophet proclaims that the sentinels lift up their voices and sing for joy. We are invited to join the chorus and sing, rejoicing at God's powerful in-breaking into our lives.

Our text from Hebrews 1:1-4 lifts up the name that is above every name, the Son of God, the reflection of the divine, Jesus. Our text for the day is both a background check, recalling God speaking to the saints of old, and an identity confirmation that this Child is the Son of God. Even the angels worship him.

And, at last, the Word becomes flesh. John 1:1-14 pushes us to move from the cradle to one through whom all things were created. He is the light shining in the darkness that illumines our way and lights our inner candles so that we might shine and testify regarding him. I invite you today as you read and meditate on the passages to lift your hands, open your heart, and sing with me—oh come let us adore him, oh come let us adore him, oh come let us adore him, Christ the Lord!

THANK GOD FOR THE MESSAGE AND THE MESSENGER
ISAIAH 52:7-10

One of my favorite parts of worship is liturgical dancing. I am always enthralled at the mix of music, interpretive movement, joy, and the Spirit. The dancers range in age from very young—maybe six years old—to young adults. There is always an air of excitement and anticipation as they enter the sanctuary to render their offering in dance. I often wonder, as I look at the thin, black leather slippers they wear, why their feet do not hurt or get injured in what appear to be such fragile shoes. They jump and twirl and contort their feet with almost every move, yet they seem un-phased by the movements. I realize that years of dancing have toughened their feet and perhaps lessened the sensitivity of their soles to the point that their feet can easily facilitate the various moments of dance. I imagine, too, that after such intense pounding of the feet that their feet must be sweaty from the sheer energy, force, and rapidity of movement. I am equally enthralled by the interpretative movement of their arms. They have long, strong, often bare arms that tell the story almost by themselves. The leanness and musculature of their arms reflect the hours of hard work done in preparation for this time of praise. It seems to me that the dancers have a celestial choreographer because the joy, the meaning, the intensity, or the softness of the movements of their arms and hands communicate so well the words of the songs to which they are dancing. It is amazing to me that the dancers' feet, arms, hands, and bodies are instruments of praise that communicate celebration, joy, and the good news.

Christmas Day is a day of celebration, of praise for the coming of our Lord. As I read our lectionary text for today from Isaiah, I envisioned the "feet of a messenger." I saw the tiny feet of Jesus, born as a baby in a manger. I wondered if methodically it would be correct to say it was a breech birth—feet first. This imagery comes to mind in light of the generations of trials and struggles of God's people before the Advent of the Christ Child. Israel's labor pains of exile, destruction, disobedience, and repentance are now replaced with the long-awaited Messiah. Though born in travail, the feet of the long-awaited Messiah are, nonetheless, "happy feet" for Israel and for us. I love the animated movie *Happy Feet*. It tells the story of the little penguin who could not sing like all the other penguins of his clan, but when he heard music or wanted to express his joy, his feet would just start moving and dancing to the music. He would get "happy feet." Everyone and everything

around him changed, got happy, and cel⟨...⟩
And his rhythm was contagious to most. S⟨...⟩
out in a joyful dance similar to his. They⟨...⟩
and experiencing the joy the little pengu⟨...⟩
fellow penguins was that one can be "differ⟨...⟩
instrument of joy.

The feet of the Savior are good news, "happy feet" for break⟨...⟩
think I have ever seen a Nativity scene with the feet of baby Jesus.
Yet Christians liken Jesus to the messenger in Isaiah whose beautiful feet ru⟨...⟩
to spread peace, good news, and salvation. Isaiah's depiction is a reminder
to pause at the side of the manger with Mary and Joseph to examine and
rejoice over the messenger sent from God who is also the message.

Isaiah also affords us another opportunity to recall the joyous good news
of Christ's birth. We break into song with the angels and stand in awe with
the shepherds that this Child is the seed of promise for our lives and for the
world. And the even greater news is that the Baby in the manger is not the
end of the story. The fact that the Savior has come as a babe in a manger is
only part of the good news of Christmas. The good news is embodied in his
life, death, and Resurrection, as well as his promise to come again for the
church. Jesus' life and ministry provided for us a message of hope for a sin
sick world. Jesus demonstrated for us the message of how to live, to teach, to
preach, to minister to our neighbors, and to serve God. How amazing it is
that Jesus is both the *messenger* of peace, justice, and righteousness and the
message of repentance and salvation available to all.

Isaiah juxtaposes the beautiful feet of the messenger with the bare arm
of the Holy One (verse 10). What a beautiful picture of tenderness and
strength, endurance and power, mercy and justice. Our God reigns! Our
God is in control of our circumstances and situations. There is no God like
our God who rejoices *with us* and flexes muscles *for us* when necessary. The
incarnated presence of God was manifested in Jesus' power and passion for
his people. Jesus Christ is the Prince of Peace and the King of kings. He is
the Lamb of God (gentle and teachable) and the Lion of the tribe of Judah
(majestic and powerful). He is Mary's baby and her Savior. He became our
sin to provide for us salvation. God's bare arm depicts strength, power, and
might on our behalf juxtaposed with God's gentleness, mercy, and kindness
fulfilled in Christ Jesus.

Jesus Christ is the messenger born in a stable so that he might proclaim
the good news of salvation that is available to all. The nails in his feet and
hands, and the sword in his side, were for our liberation. We are free to
dance with happy feet the praises of our journey empowered by a God who
is "strong and powerful...powerful in battle" (Psalm 24:8). A God who is
constantly at work on our behalf. We can sing the songs of Zion, even in

know the victory is already won. We can proclaim
us is coming back again.

d of the sermon, the pastor would say, "Let's bless God for
nd the Messenger." That statement takes on new meaning for
s Christmas Day. It refers not just to the preparation and delivery
sermon. Nor is it just an accolade to the preacher who just preached.
e larger message is that we are to thank God for the message proclaimed
by Jesus Christ and proclaimed by the saints down through the centuries.
And we are to thank God for the messenger, Jesus Christ. Without Jesus'
birth, death, and resurrection, Christmas would be an ordinary day in the
life cycle of humanity filled with commercialism and food. Praise be to God
for the Message and the Messenger!

*As you reflect on this Christmas morning, what makes your feet happy and causes you
to praise God? How has God been strong on your behalf during this year?*

WHEN MYSTERY MEETS THE MUNDANE
HEBREWS 1:1-4 (5-12)

Our family has a tradition that we engage in every Christmas. Before we
open any presents, we sit as a family and reflect on who Jesus is in our lives and
what the birth of the Christ Child means to us. We each share at least one new
insight that we have gained during the year about the power and promise of
Christ in our lives. As a child, I did not like this tradition. Mom would have to
get her coffee, and everyone would come together in the family room where
all the gifts were staring me in the face, taking what seemed to be an eternity
to gather. I would think to myself, "here we go with the Jesus stuff again. Just
say something so we can get to Christmas." I wanted to tear into my presents,
throw wrapping paper all over the floor, and have fun with my gifts.

I recall one Christmas when the beautiful, pink bike that I wanted was
sitting in the middle of the family room floor. So before our ritual, I ran
and sat on the bike. Mama asked me what I was doing. I promptly said
I was getting ready so I could ride on the King's highway! She did not find
my antics amusing. For my mother, it seemed that the reflective tradition
was the highlight of the day. Even now, I can see the look of peace and
contentment on her face as she sipped her coffee and listened to each
reflection. Sometimes she would shed a tear of joy over a comment made by
a family member. She did not seem to be interested in the material gifts. It
appeared to me that the gift she valued was hearing us share God's activity
in our lives and the deepening of our relationship with Jesus. Today, we are
invited to take a reflective pause to open and examine the greatest gift ever

given to us, Jesus Christ. Christmas Day b...
who Jesus is and how his coming into the...
lives and the whole of humanity.

Hebrews 1:1-12 is both a background chec...
It juxtaposes Jesus' divinity and his humanit...
identity of Jesus. The writer sets the record straigh...
ordinary child. Heaven and earth worship him. His nam...
other name. We get a look at the celestial, prenatal and human, ...
Messiah through the poetic melody of this text about the Baby born superio...
to angels (verse 4).

If you have ever witnessed a baby being born, you know it is one of the most miraculous events of life. It is a medical marvel to see a miniature human being emerge into the world. All the months of waiting, all the hours of preparation, and even the excruciating pain of labor, all melt away with that first cry of the long anticipated one. Joy fills the room. Even the nurses and the doctors are smiling and giving thanks for the tiny medical marvel. What a wonderful occasion it is for everyone. The new parents have hopes and dreams and aspirations for that child. The dad may have already purchased a baseball glove. The mom has imagined her daughter going to college, getting married, and having her own children. It is a time of hope and promise coalescing into the activities of daily living.

As hopeful as parents are, we often do not realize that we may have given birth to the next Nelson Mandela, Sojourner Truth, Dr. Martin Luther King Jr., John Wesley, or Jonas Salk. While we hope for the best for that child, we usually do not know or have a clear idea of how his or her life will influence the world. Will this child make a difference in society and be a contributing member to peace, justice, hope, and the betterment of the world? In what way will this child's presence in the world make a difference? How can I, as a parent, godparent, relative, or friend be an influence for good in this child's life? These are but a few of the questions that loom large in our hearts as we greet this new human into our small circles.

Mary and Joseph must have had similar questions swirling in their heads on the night of Jesus' birth. Even though the angel of the Lord had appeared to Mary and told her that her child, conceived by the Holy Spirit, would be great and be given a kingdom that has no end (Luke 1:26-38), the full import of that statement was yet to unfold. The mystery that she had pondered in her heart was born. Centuries after the birth of the Christ Child, songwriter Mark Lowry captured the intersection of the Word and the world in a brilliantly simple song written for a Christmas play at his church. Lowry asks a series of questions that elucidate the fact that this was no ordinary child, who would live an ordinary life, or even die an ordinary death. His song speaks directly to Mary about the wonder and awe of bearing the Christ Child. He begins

ful song with its title, "Mary Did You Know," then
nd the mystery of the Baby born King.[2] Lowry inspires
manger with Mary and Joseph and reflect upon what God
ough the birth of Jesus. When Mary's water broke and gushed
body, she probably did not understand that this Child would one
peak to the winds and the waves to calm the storms and, one day, walk
n water. This Child that she delivered would one day be her deliverer. This
tiny miracle would one day give sight to the blind, make the lame walk, and
heal all manner of diseases. This Baby, born in a stable among the animals,
would be called "the Lamb of God" (John 1:29) and the "Lion of the tribe
of Judah" (Revelation 5:5). For me, the most beautiful and powerful lines in
the song reverberate through history. Lowry asked Mary:

Did you know that your baby boy has walked where angels trod?
And when your kiss your little baby, you have kissed the face of God.

These two lines capture the power of God's mystery meeting the mundane
existence of humanity. Out of the darkness of the womb bursts forth the
light of the world. This baby is the long-awaited Messiah, and yet he is the
first over all creation (Colossians 1:15). He is the author of creation and
the image of the invisible God. Mary did not know that this Child would
be crucified on a cross for political insurrection and also, one day, be the
ruler of all nations. Jesus asks us today, do you know who I am? I am love
personified for you. I am the light that expels the darkness of living. I am the
mystery of your faith, the one who was born, who died, who was raised, and
who will come again.

What song expresses for you the mystery and majesty of Christ's birth? What new
insight did you gain this year about who Jesus is in your life? Find a YouTube version
of the song "Mary Did You Know," and take time to reflect on the words and their
meaning in your life.

BEHOLD THE LIGHT
JOHN 1:1-14

The Prologue of John's Gospel evokes so much imagery for us on this
Christmas Day. It is as if we are children in a toy store trying to decide which
exhilarating object we should explore first. In these first fourteen verses we
are introduced to the incarnate God, the Creator, the life, the light, the
children born of God, the rejecters of the light, and the witnesses to the
light. Among these profound images of John's Gospel is the image of light
that fractures all darkness though the Word that has become flesh. The

cosmos yields to "the one who is and was and who is coming" (Revelation 1:4). The imagery of the Word putting on flesh and breaking into human history is a source of hope and joy for us today. The Word through which all things were created has come to save all of creation from its darkness. The Word is the "light of the world" that was with God in the beginning and is God and has come to bring us life and light.

Paul Lee Tan writes in "The Nature of Light," *Encyclopedia of 7000 Illustrations: Signs of the Times* that light is constituted in three rays or three groups of wavelengths. These three wavelengths are distinct from each other; no one of which without the others would be light. Each ray has a separate function from the other rays, yet the three are one. Scientists believe that the function of the first ray is to originate, to be the initiator of bringing "light" into being. It is called the invisible light because it is not felt or seen, but evidence suggests that it is there. The second ray illuminates. This ray is both seen and felt—there is no question of its presence because the evidence and impact of this ray is undeniable. The third ray consummates. This ray is not seen, but its presence is undeniable because it is felt as heat.[3] This trinitarian motif (three in one) about the nature of light may be helpful to appreciate the theological depth of the statement that the Word is the true light.

This motif offers an excellent way to think about the unity and continuity of the relationship between God and the Word, our source of light as described in John's Prologue. Like the first ray, God is invisible; we cannot see God. The Scripture says that God is a Spirit and those who worship God must worship in Spirit and truth. We cannot see God but all of creation witnesses to God's creative work and life. The Genesis narrative simply says, "in the beginning God created" (Genesis 1:1, KJV). God's invisible qualities are understood through the things made by God (see Romans 1:20). The Word in John's Prologue was present in the beginning with God creating, radiating, and even then, providing for us.

Like the second ray of light, the Word was both seen and felt. John reminds us this Christmas morning that God took on flesh and made his home among us, so humanity could see and feel God. On Christmas Eve, we kneel beside the manger to behold the Christ Child, to celebrate the long-awaited Baby born to save the world. But our reading from John moves us to celebrate the pre-existent Word, the one who loved us so much that he came as an example of how to overcome the darkness with his light. The darkness of the world—disbelief, wars, crime, and even death—are overcome by the true light—our Savior. Light extinguishes the darkness, so we can be fearless in the face of uncertainty. As we read Scripture, we see the works of the Word, and we feel his presence day by day as we travel trough life. The word is a lamp to our feet and a light for our journey (Psalm 119:105).

And, like that third ray, when we make that personal connection with God, we can't see God but we experience the heat, the fire of God's presence. I don't know about you, but sometimes when I think about the goodness of God, sending the Son, Jesus, the Word made flesh, my palms start to sweat, my forehead perspires, and my feet start tapping as the fire of divine grace engulfs me. Like Jeremiah, there is a fire shut up in my bones (Jeremiah 20:9). And like John, I must testify to the light and the life made available to us through Jesus Christ.

Robert Louis Stevenson, author of *Treasure Island*, suffered from poor health during most of his childhood and youth. It is reported that one night, his nurse found him with his nose pressed against the frosty pane of his bedroom window. "Child, come away from there. You'll catch your death of cold," she insisted. Young Robert did not move. He sat mesmerized as he watched an old lamplighter slowly working his way through the black night, lighting each street lamp along his route. Pointing his fingers in sheer excitement, Robert exclaimed, "See; look there; there's a man poking holes in the darkness."[4]

The Word came to humanity and demonstrated and empowered us to "poke holes in the darkness" of the world. As John noted, we are not the true light, rather, we are to testify to and reflect his light. Jesus, the true light, admonished us, his followers, to let our light shine before people so they can see the good works we do and praise our God in heaven (Matthew 5:16). We are not to diminish or extinguish our light. We are children of God who are to manifest the light of God within. Jesus, our Savior, the Word that became flesh, shattered the darkness that we might overcome darkness and experience life and light. Behold the light, Jesus Christ.

In what ways does creation testify to the creative involvement of Jesus Christ in the world and in your life? What is your testimony of new light that was shed upon you this Advent season? How might you more fully walk in the light of Christ in your home, in your job, in your church, and in your social life this coming year?

1. First coined by Ada Maria Isasi-Diaz. She uses the term "kin-dom of God" rather than the hierarchal, sexist term Kingdom. She says Kin-dom "makes it clear that when the fullness of God becomes a day-to-day reality in the world at large, we will all be sisters and brothers–kin to each other" (304). "Solidarity: Love of Neighbor in the 1980s," by Ada Maria Isasi-Diaz, in *Lift Every Voice: Constructing Christian Theologies from the Underside,* edited by Susan Brooks Thistlethwaite and Mary Potter Engel (Harper, 1990); pages 31-40, 303-305.

2. See *http://www.lyricsmode.com/lyrics/m/mark_lowry/mary_did_you_know.html*; Lyrics written by Mark Lowry, Warner/ Chappel Music Inc., 1984.
3. From "The Nature of Light" in *Encyclopedia of 7000 Illustrations: Signs of the Times*, by Paul Lee Tan (Assurance Publishers, 1979); page 740.
4. See *http://www.preaching.com/common-lectionary/11700523/*.

$\mathscr{L}$eader Guide

HOW TO LEAD THIS STUDY

The Lord Is Our Light invites adults to explore and reflect upon the Revised Common Lectionary Bible readings for the season of Advent. This Advent study is rooted in the texts for Year B of the three-year lectionary cycle of readings. Each week you will find readings from the Old Testament, the Epistles, and a Gospel. "How to Lead This Study" guides you in setting up and leading the study. You'll discover tips for preparing for each week's session, as well as ideas about how to successfully lead a Bible study, even if you have never led one before. Although the Revised Common Lectionary designates a psalm or words of praise for each week, they are generally not discussed in the main content. These additional Scriptures are, however, listed here for your convenience. "How to Lead This Study" offers some historical and theological information about the season of Advent and suggests ways that people now and in different times and places have observed this sacred time. In addition, you will find prayers and a selection of hymns appropriate for each week's session.

About Advent

Advent is the first season in the twelve-month cycle of seasons in the church known as the liturgical year. The word *advent* is from a Latin word that means coming. This definition is fitting, for during the season of Advent we await the coming of Christ. We look in two directions for this coming: backward in time to recall the birth of Jesus Christ in Bethlehem and forward as we anticipate his return. In Western churches the season begins four weeks prior to Christmas on the Sunday closest to November 30th and ends on Christmas Eve. Altars have traditionally been adorned in purple, the color of royalty that reminds us of Christ's sovereignty. Purple is also associated with penitence, which is appropriate for this season because historically, Advent, like Lent, has been a time to reflect and repent. More recently, blue has been favored in many churches because of its association with Mary, whom artists often depict wearing blue. Just as Mary waited for the birth of her holy Child, so the church eagerly awaits his coming.

Advent is a time of preparation. However, some churches rush headlong into Christmas, skipping over this important time to get ready. Even on the first week of Advent, Christmas carols ring out. Nativity scenes feature the magi, whose arrival is celebrated on January 6th, which is Epiphany. On the church calendar, the Christmas season begins with the birth of Jesus and ends with Epiphany. Although the secular world may push us toward Christmas, in the church we take the time to prepare ourselves for Christ's coming and coming again.

Advent has the potential to form and transform us if we allow that to happen. As we wait expectantly for the One God called Son, we bump up against the realities of the world with all its suffering, injustice, and hostility. Yet if we consider the scriptural promises of this season, we know that God is at work among us and within us to change not only ourselves but also the world. We live in the space between the first and second coming of Christ. God's realm has broken in upon us with Jesus' birth; it will appear in its fullness when he returns. In the interim, we live as Advent people who keep alert and constantly prepare for his coming.

Ways to Celebrate Advent

The season of Advent provides time for us to get ready for the coming—and coming again—of our Lord Jesus Christ. During this season of preparation, many people attend special study groups, just as you are doing, to discover what the Savior's coming is all about and what he means in their lives. People use Advent wreaths and Advent calendars as two means of personal spiritual growth. Another way to celebrate the season, setting up an angel tree, involves sharing resources with those in need.

ADVENT WREATHS: Many sanctuaries, Sunday school rooms, and homes are adorned with Advent wreaths. Thought to have first been used in northern Europe, wreath traditions have varied; but by the sixteenth century, the wreath had taken on the form that we recognize today. The roundness of the wreath and the evergreens used to create it symbolize life. Traditionally, three purple candles are lit on the first, second, and fourth Sundays. A rose-colored candle, symbolizing joy, is lit on the third Sunday. More recently, blue candles are used for all four weeks. Some wreaths include a center white candle, which is lit late on Christmas Eve to symbolize Christ.

ADVENT CALENDARS: Originating in Germany in the late 1800's, Advent calendars provide a way to count down the days until Christmas, beginning on December 1. The calendar includes 24 small windows, and each window hides a picture. Although early calendars used images from the Old Testament, contemporary ones frequently display items appealing to children, such as teddy bears or candy.

ANGEL TREES: Some churches and other organizations decorate trees using angels, which are often made of construction paper. Listed on the angels are items that an individual or family in need would like to have for Christmas. Generally these lists include food, clothing (with sizes and colors indicated), and toys. Lists are usually provided by social-services agencies or schools. Those who choose to participate select an angel, purchase the requested items, and return them by the date specified on the angel. Some organizations ask that the gifts be wrapped; others prefer to wrap all gifts in a central location. Either way, gifts need to be marked using the number or code shown on the angel. A group of helpers delivers the gifts, usually on December 23rd or 24th.

Organize an Advent Study Group

Advent is an especially busy time of year for most people. Yet, it is also a time when Christians yearn to deepen their relationship with Christ. Study groups are an excellent way to enable people to delve deeper into the Bible and to reach out in friendship to others. Established groups—Sunday school classes, current Bible study groups, men's or women's groups—may choose to focus on Advent. Also consider forming a new group for this five-week Advent study. By advertising the study in local media, you can open wide the doors of the church to include those from other congregations—or no congregation at all.

When you, in conjunction with the pastor and church education team, have determined the shape of the group, decide when and where the group can meet. An established group would most likely continue to meet in its regular space and time. A new group will have to be scheduled so as not to conflict with other activities that potential participants would likely attend, such as choir rehearsal. Evening meetings are more likely to pull in individuals who are still working, whereas daytime meetings may be more attractive to older adults who choose not to be out after dark, full-time moms, and perhaps college students. The time of the meeting will suggest whether refreshments are needed. A Saturday morning is a good time to offer a continental breakfast. A noon meeting could include the invitation to bring a bag lunch. An evening meeting might include some light snacks and beverages.

The learning space should be large enough for the group you anticipate. A Sunday school room with tables would be ideal. Since many churches conserve energy by regulating individual room temperatures, request that the room be properly heated by the time the participants arrive and remain so during the meeting time. Make sure that a small worship table and large writing surface, such as an easel with large sheets of paper and markers, a whiteboard with markers, or a blackboard with chalk will be on hand. Have a separate space available and a designated worker to provide childcare.

Decide whether you want to hold a preregistration. Whether you do or not, be sure to order enough copies of *The Lord Is Our Light* so that each participant has the study book. The church will need to determine how much to charge participants or whether to underwrite the cost and announce that the study is free.

Prepare for the Sessions

Leading a Bible study is a sacred privilege. Before you begin the "nuts and bolts" work, pray for the Holy Spirit to guide you and the participants as you encounter each week's Bible passages. Try reading each Scripture devotionally by asking God to speak to your heart through a word or phrase that grabs your attention. Meditate on whatever you are shown and allow this idea to shape your own spiritual growth.

Read the Scriptures and Bible Background for each week's lesson to understand the context of the Scriptures and their meaning. If time permits, consult other commentaries to expand your knowledge. Once you feel comfortable with the Scriptures, begin to plan the session by following these steps:

1. Read the chapter for the week from *The Lord Is Our Light.*
2. Refer to the Session Plan where you will find suggested activities that will help the participants engage the Scripture and activities to open the session and to close the session. Be aware that the activities generally include discussion, but some include art, music, movement, or other means of learning in addition to discussion.
3. When activities refer directly to *The Lord Is Our Light,* mark the places in your book for easy reference during the session.
4. Gather supplies needed for each activity.
5. Select any hymn(s) you wish to use. If you will sing the hymn(s), notify your accompanist.
6. Determine how you will use the lectionary psalm or other additional reading.
7. Contact any guest speakers or assistants early in the week if you will use their services.

Helpful Ideas for Leading A Group

Bible studies come in many shapes, sizes, and formats. Some begin with a theme and find biblical support for it. Others begin with the Bible itself and unpack the Scriptures, whether from one book or several. Our study begins with the Bible, specifically the texts of the Revised Common Lectionary. Those Scriptures will deeply inform our study. However, *The Lord Is Our Light* is not a "verse by verse" study of the readings. Instead, we are studying the texts as a kind of road map to guide us in our spiritual journey through the Advent season. Consequently, some of the suggested activities call participants to struggle with questions of faith in their own lives. Our focus is primarily on transformation so that participants may grow in their relationship with Jesus Christ and become more closely conformed to his image. That's a tall order for a five-week course! And it may be somewhat challenging for the participants, since it may be far easier to discuss historical information about the Bible and consider various interpretations of a passage than it is to wrestle with what the passage says to me—personally and as a member of the body of Christ—in contemporary life.

Your role as the leader of this group is to create an environment in which participants will feel safe in raising their questions and expressing their doubts. You can also help the class feel comfortable by making clear that you rely solely on volunteers to answer questions and to read aloud. If adults feel pressed to respond or read, they may be embarrassed and may not return to the group. If questions arise that you can definitely answer, do so. If you do not know the answer but suspect that an answer is available, say you do not know and offer to look it up and report back at the next session. Or, suggest a type of resource that will likely include the answer and challenge the questioner and others to do some research and report back. Some questions cannot be fully answered—at least not in this life. Do not be afraid to point out that people through the ages have wrestled with some questions and yet they remain mysteries. If you can truly say so, respond that you have wrestled with that same question and have found an answer that works for you, or that you are still searching. When you show yourself to be a co-learner, the participants will feel more comfortable than if you act as the all-knowing expert. You will feel more at ease about leading the group as well.

Additional Scriptures for Advent

The additional Scriptures for this season come from the Psalms. Suggestions are given in some of the sessions for using these Scriptures, but you may want to try other options. For example, consider reading each psalm responsively, possibly adding the sung response if you are using the Psalter in your hymnal. Note that on the fourth Sunday of Advent, Mary's song of praise in Luke replaces the psalm.

First Sunday of Advent: Psalm 80:1-7, 17-19
Second Sunday of Advent: Psalm 85:1-2, 8-13
Third Sunday of Advent: Psalm 126
Fourth Sunday of Advent: Luke 1:47-55
Christmas Day: Psalm 98

1. Mindful Waiting

BIBLE BACKGROUND*

During Advent, the first season of the Christian calendar, the church looks to the coming of both the incarnate Jesus, the Son of God who was born to Mary, and the cosmic Christ who will come again in glory on the day of the Lord. On the first Sunday of Advent, the church focuses attention on Christ's coming again. Today's reading from Isaiah reminds us that God has saved people from their sinfulness in the past and can be counted on to do so again. First Corinthians points toward the day of the Lord and assures believers that God will sustain them so that they will be "blameless"[1] on that day. In Mark, we overhear Jesus teaching the disciples about his return and urging them to be watchful and alert for his coming, since no one except the Father knows when that transformational event will occur.

Isaiah 64:1-9

This passage is part of a long community lament that begins at 63:7 and continues through 64:12.[2] In this lament,[3] the Israelite community reminded God of God's gracious acts of redemption in the Exodus (63:8-9), the people's rebellions in the wilderness (verses 10-13a), and the settlement in the Promised Land (verses 13b-14).[4] The people wanted to know where God was, because they needed God to redeem them again.

In 64:1-3, the Israelites called upon God to "tear open the heavens" and powerfully intervene in human history with "wonders beyond all [their] expectations" (verse 3), as of old. The people acknowledged that God acts on behalf of those who do what is right. However, the Israelites confessed that they had sinned, prompting God to hide from them and hand them over to their sin (verse 7).

In the throes of their distress, the people were still confident that God, who is their "father" and has fashioned them as a potter (verse 8), would set aside fierce rage and look on them with favor. And so they implored God not to "hold [their] sins against [them] forever" (verse 9).[5]

These verses follow the typical pattern of a lament: the people cry out for God to redeem them (verses 1-4); they describe their distressing situation (verses 5-7); they affirm their confidence in God (verse 8); and they request God's favor (verse 9).

Isaiah 64:1-9 is a fitting way to begin this season of Advent. The Israelites felt alienated from God because of their sinfulness. They recognized that God would have to act in power to redeem them again, just as in ages past. Similarly, in the first century A.D. God intervened in human history to redeem sinful people by becoming incarnate in the person of Jesus Christ. Humans had no hope of reconciling themselves to God, but God's merciful, gracious action in sending Emmanuel, God with us, could indeed bridge the chasm and redeem humans from their sinfulness.

1 Corinthians 1:3-9

After identifying himself as an apostle and greeting the saints in Corinth, Paul extended to them the grace and peace of God the Father and Jesus Christ the Lord. Following his usual pattern of greeting, Paul then offered a prayer for the congregation in Corinth (verses 4-9). Since letters were typically read aloud during a congregational gathering, Paul's opening greeting and prayer established an appropriate mood for worship.

His prayer sets the tone and agenda for everything else he will discuss in this letter. Paul rooted his message in God's gracious gift of Christ (verse 4). The apostle reminded the believers that they were not only rich in "communication" and "knowledge" (verse 5), but they also did not lack for any spiritual gift (verse 7). Moreover, they could rest assured that God would faithfully sustain them until "the day of our Lord" (verse 8). As verse 9 makes clear, God is the one who takes the initiative to call believers into a relationship with Jesus. They enter into fellowship with him and, as this letter will later demonstrate, with other members of his body.

Paul's emphasis on spiritual gifts here is explored later in the letter. Some members of the church seemed to feel inferior to those who were more experienced Christians and apparently had stronger credentials in the faith. Chapter 12, in particular, makes clear that each member has a gift and a vital role to play in the body of Christ. Paul will also later stress the faithfulness of God, who called them into the body and would sustain them until the end.

This passage from 1 Corinthians 1 helps us to enter into the season of Advent by highlighting the church's need to wait for the revealing of the Lord (verse 7) and God's faithfulness in sustaining believers so that when the day of the Lord does arrive they will be found "blameless" (verse 8).

Mark 13:24-37

Commentators often refer to Mark 13 as "the little Apocalypse"[6] because its themes and images are similar to those in the apocalyptic literature such as the Book of Revelation. In Mark's Gospel, Jesus was teaching his disciples (verse 1) about future events. Jesus began his lesson with a foretelling of the destruction of the Temple, which did occur in AD 70, nearly forty years after Jesus' crucifixion. Jesus also warned the disciples that they would be persecuted, before turning his attention to the coming of the Son of Man that will follow their torment.

In verses 24-27, Jesus described the celestial upheaval that would occur just prior to the return of "the Human One…with great power and splendor" (verse 26). At his coming, angels will traverse the earth to gather believers. Jesus told the parable of the fig tree (verses 28-31) to help his listeners understand that, just as the sprouting of tree leaves signifies that summer is near at hand, so there will be signs of his Coming. He went on to say that only the Father knew exactly when the end would come. Jesus implied that it was futile for his followers to try to guess the time. Rather, they should be watchful and alert at all times. The section concludes in verses 34-37 with another parable urging the disciples not only to be alert but also to be doing what they were called to do. Jesus spoke of an owner who went on an extended trip and left his household under the care of his servants. The date and time of his return were unknown, but the master had admonished them to be alert and ready for his return at any time of the day or night. Jesus warned the disciples not to be sleeping when the householder returned. Certainly, they should be about the master's business when he returns and not neglecting their duties.

During Advent, we prepare with eager anticipation to welcome Jesus as we commemorate his birth and continue to await his Second Coming.

SESSION PLAN

Open the Session

Set the stage for this study.

Welcome participants. Distribute the text, *The Lord Is Our Light.* Encourage participants to read the Scriptures and text prior to each week's session. Recommend that they bring their Bible, study book, paper, and a pencil or pen each week.

Tend to housekeeping matters, such as restroom locations and book payment.

Enlist a volunteer to read aloud the first portion of "Mindful Waiting." Distribute paper and pencils, and encourage participants to reflect on and write answers to these questions that you will read aloud:

1. What new beginnings do you hope to make during this Advent season?
2. How do you expect this study to help you make these new beginnings?
3. In what ways are you now experiencing God's love and grace? (pause)

Suggest that participants refer to their answers each week of Advent to identify new beginnings they have made in their spiritual journeys.

Offer an opening prayer.

Holy One, may our hearts and minds stay focused on Jesus as we await his coming as God with us and his coming again as the King of kings and Lord of lords. Amen.

Engage the Scriptures

Encounter Isaiah 64:1-9.

Introduce this passage by reading or summarizing the Bible Background for this Scripture.

Choose two volunteers who have the same Bible translation to read alternating verses of Isaiah 64:1-9.

Form two groups and assign one of the following questions, which you will write on a large sheet of paper, to each group. Suggest that the groups use their Bibles and the section "Blame or Blessing" to help answer the questions:

1. What do you learn about who God is and what God has done?
2. What do you learn about the Israelites and their relationship with God?

Reunite the groups and call on a spokesperson from each group to report highlights of their discussion. Conclude by asking: How does this passage from Isaiah help you understand the relationship between God and Israel?

Write a litany.

Solicit a volunteer to read Isaiah 64:1-9.

Ask someone else to read "Blame or Blessing," beginning with "Israel's behavior and prayers" through to the end.

Distribute slips of paper and pencils. Ask participants to write one action or attitude for which they need to repent. Pass around a basket or other container to collect the folded slips of paper. Pass the container around again; this time each person is to take out one slip of paper. In turn, participants will read what is written on the slip of paper they pulled out. You will list each action or attitude on a large sheet of paper.

Read this list as a litany. One person will read the first item, to which the group will respond, "Help us to turn around and begin anew, O God." The next person will read the second item and the group will respond. Continue until all the actions and attitudes have been included.

Explore 1 Corinthians 1:3-9.

Select a volunteer to read Paul's salutation and prayer of thanksgiving from 1 Corinthians 1:3-9. Invite the participants to listen as if they were members of the church in Corinth.

Suggest that participants read silently the Bible Background for this Scripture passage to discern the purpose of these verses and how they relate to the rest of Paul's letter.

Discuss these questions from the point of view of the Corinthian believers:

1. Knowing that your congregation has a reputation for conflict, how would Paul's words of thanksgiving have made you feel? *hopeful*
2. How would you have responded to Paul's comment that "you aren't missing any spiritual gift" (verse 7)? *comforting + confidence building*
3. How do you experience God's faithfulness to you and to your church?

Identify Christian behaviors.

Call on a volunteer to read the first and second paragraph of "Seriously?"

Post a large sheet of paper and encourage participants to identify types of behaviors they see Christians engage in. Read the items on the list, one at a time, and ask, "Seriously, does a Christian do that?" Some items will reflect appropriate behavior and should be commended. If an item does not reflect the participants' expectations of how Christians should behave, probe to find out why this particular behavior is not suitable—and how that behavior needs to be changed or eliminated.

End this activity by discussing ways in which behaviors—both those that are appropriate and those that are not—affect the witness of an individual Christian within the church and the church's corporate witness within the community.

Discover Jesus' teachings in Mark 13:24-37.

Read aloud the first paragraph of the Bible Background for Mark 13:24-37.

Note that this passage is divided into three parts. Choose a volunteer to read each part: Mark 13:24-27, 28-31, 32-37. Discuss these questions:

1. How will the cosmos respond to the second coming of Christ?
2. Jesus said he would come again, and that there would be signs of his coming. But he also said that only God knew when that time would be. What does his teaching suggest to you about how you are to live in the meantime?

3. In what ways is your congregation staying alert and tending to the household of God?

Discern how to live with the end in mind.

Point out that in Mark 13:24-37 Jesus was teaching us how to live with the end in mind. Call on a volunteer to read this passage. Note that the end to which Jesus refers is the day of the Lord, the end of the age as we know it.

Choose someone to read the first and second paragraphs of "Begin with the End in Mind."

Encourage participants to tell brief stories of how they envisioned and achieved results related to certain goals they had set for themselves.

Form pairs or teams of three and post these discussion questions on a large sheet of paper:

1. What goal do you want to achieve by the end of this Advent season?
2. How will you make that happen?
3. What signs of change in your life do you anticipate seeing?
4. What will you do to keep alert for the presence of Jesus in your life right now?

Close the Session

Reflect on today's encounter with the Scripture.

Invite participants to meditate on these questions, which you will read slowly, allowing time for reflection:

1. How have these Scriptures helped you to enter into the meaning of Advent? (pause)
2. Which passage do you want to delve into more deeply? Why? (pause)
3. What actions do you feel compelled to take as a result of studying today's Scriptures? (pause)

Offer a closing prayer.

Point out that Psalm 80, like today's reading from Isaiah 64, is a lament by the entire community.[7] In this Psalm, the people appeal to the "Shepherd of Israel" (verse 1) to "restore" them so that they "can be saved" (verses 3, 7, 19).

Suggest that this psalm be the participants' prayer as they begin Advent by recognizing their own sinfulness and calling on God to restore and save them.

Ask one volunteer to read verses 1-2, 4-6, and 17-18. Invite all participants to read in unison the refrain found in verses 3, 7, and 19.

* Possible references consulted; footnotes refer to first editor's name or NIB or NISB: *Eerdmans Dictionary of the Bible*, edited by David Noel Freedman; *Feasting on the Word, Year B*, Volume 1, edited by David L. Bartlett and Barbara Brown Taylor; *Preaching Through the Christian Year, Year B*, edited by Fred B. Craddock, Carl R. Holladay, Gene M. Tucker; *The New Interpreter's Bible* ; and *The New Interpreter's Study Bible*.

   1. From CEB; 1 Corinthians 1:8.
   2. From NIB, Volume VI; page 524, left column.
   3. From NISB; page 1044, footnote for 63:7–64:12.
   4. From NISB; page 1044, footnote for 63:7-14.
   5. From *Preaching Through the Christian Year, Year B*, edited by Fred B. Craddock, Carl R. Holladay, Gene M. Tucker; pages 1-2.
   6. From NISB; page 1835, footnote for 13:1-37.
   7. From NISB; page 823, footnote for 80:1-19.

2. Expectant Preparation

BIBLE BACKGROUND*

This week's Scriptures sound a brighter note than last week's readings. We have moved from the lament of the people and Jesus' teaching about the end of time to the good news that he is coming soon to comfort and redeem those who wait for the Lord. But when will Christ return? Peter's second letter addressed the concerns of those early church members who awaited Christ. Since he had not yet come, their hopes dimmed as they wondered if he would come at all.

As is true in all three years of the Revised Common Lectionary cycle, the person and proclamation of John the Baptist, also called John the Baptizer, is highlighted in the Gospel passages on the second Sunday of Advent.[1] He played a major role in bridging the gap between the two testaments as the Elijah-like prophet who prepared people for the immediate arrival of the Messiah.

Isaiah 40:1-11

Chapter 40 marks a turning point in the prophecy of Isaiah. Whereas scholars attribute most of Chapters 1–39 to one known as Isaiah of Jerusalem,[2] Chapters 40–55 are oracles from about 540 BC that a prophet referred to as Second Isaiah spoke to assure the exiles in Babylon that God still cared for them and was ultimately in charge.

Most Israelites were forced from their homeland to Babylon in two waves: first in 597 BC and again in 586 BC when King Nebuchadnezzar's troops sacked Jerusalem and burned the Temple.[3] This terrible event occurred because the people had sinned by worshipping the gods of their neighbors and by treating the poor with contempt. They had refused to listen to prior prophets, such as Amos and Micah, and failed to change their ways. By the time that Second Isaiah prophesied, the captives felt that they were no longer God's chosen people. They doubted God's sovereignty and were in a state of despair.[4]

Isaiah's words of comfort (verse 1), assurance that the penalty for the people's sins had been paid twice over (verse 2), and that a level highway would be built for the people to return to Israel (verses 3-4) are all messages of hope for the hopeless captives. The voice that cries out this news in verse 3 is heard in all four Gospels and identified as John the Baptist.

In response to a voice calling out (verse 6), the prophet asked what he was to say. The answer is that although humans are as frail and short-lived as grass and flowers, God's Word is eternal (verses 6-8).

The good news of God is to be proclaimed from the hilltop of Zion. Verses 10-11 depict two very different images of God. In verse 10, God is portrayed as a warrior who will avenge Israel. In contrast, verse 11 shows God as the good shepherd who tenderly cares for and comforts the flock of Israel.[5]

2 Peter 3:8-15a

The author of Second Peter likely wrote in the apostle's name after his death, possibly in AD 80-90.[6] Although the letter was written to believers, it included no clues as to where it was written or to whom it was addressed. Second Peter 1:12-15 suggests that this letter was written as a farewell by one who expected his death to "come soon" (1:14, NRSV).[7] Concerned about divisions he perceived within the church, the author urged his readers to hold fast to what they had been taught and resist those false teachers who were undermining the reliability of the gospel and raising doubts that Jesus would return again.[8]

Since Christ had not yet come again, the hopes of those who were initially reading Second Peter fifty or sixty years after Jesus' crucifixion had dimmed. If he had not come by then, would he come at all? Verse 8 attempted to reframe the discussion by reminding readers that the same calendars cannot be used to measure God's time and human time. Instead of viewing the delay of Christ's return as a failure of God to keep promises, the people should see that the delay is due to divine patience as God continues to extend mercy to all who will come in repentance. Using the image of a thief (3:10), the author declared that creation would meet a fiery end.

Having warned the readers, the writer then raised the question of how people are to live in the meantime. Instead of dreading that final day, believers are admonished to be "waiting for and hastening" it (verse 12). They are not to sit by passively or behaving in any way that suits them. Instead, as they wait, they are to live "holy and godly lives" (verse 11).

As we learned last week, the belief that Christ is coming again is a major Advent theme. Like the people to whom Peter wrote, we too are to live the kind of moral and ethical lives that reflect the reconciled relationship we have with God that was made possible by Jesus.

Mark 1:1-8

The messenger who cried out in Isaiah 40 to prepare the way of the Lord is identified in Mark 1 as John the Baptist. Although all the Gospels include the person and ministry of John, Mark's account is the shortest and the earliest of the four.[9] In verse 4, John was in the wilderness calling people to repent and be baptized. Eleven verses later, John's ministry has ended with his arrest (verse 14). Mark 6:14-29 records the story of John's beheading.

Mark 1:5 reports on the popularity of John's ministry: "Everyone in Judea and all the people of Jerusalem" sought him out. They responded to his preaching by confessing their sins and being baptized. What was it that drew people to John? Mark's description in verse 6 depicts John as a prophet after Elijah (2 Kings 1:8). John's appearance and work would have reminded the people that the prophet Elijah would come "before the great and terrifying day of the LORD" (Malachi 4:5). Mark 9:11-13 also links John with Elijah. People who were awaiting the Messiah were also awaiting the return of Elijah, and John seemed to fit their expectations.

Verses 7-8 conclude this reading by quoting John's message, which not only pointed to Jesus but also indicated that the prophet was aware of his role in salvation history. He came to prepare people to hear and receive the Messiah. To that end, John proclaimed that Jesus was stronger than he was. He admitted that he was unworthy to perform even the work of a slave— untying a sandal—for Jesus.[10] John's water baptism was an important ritual for the forgiveness of sins, but Jesus' baptism with the Holy Spirit became a sign of the end times when, according to Joel 2:28-32 (quoted by Peter in his Pentecost sermon in Acts 2:17-21), God's spirit will be poured out on everyone.

SESSION PLAN

Open the Session

List Christmas Preparations.

Welcome participants back and introduce newcomers. Post a large sheet of paper on a wall or place it on a table. As participants enter the learning area, invite them to write two actions they have taken in the past week to prepare for Christmas. Have markers available so that several participants may write at the same time.

Begin the session by looking at the items listed, noting both the variety of activities and the similarities among them.

Read aloud the first paragraph of "Expectant Preparation" and ask: As you look at our list, how would you rate our spiritual preparation for the coming of the Lord? What changes might we want to make?

Read Psalm 85 as an opening prayer.

Read Psalm 85:1-2, 8-13, either responsively from the Psalter in a hymnal or in unison from the participants' Bibles. (These need not be the same translation.)

Provide a few moments of silence for the participants to consider the promises that God is making to them through this psalm and to ask the Lord to speak peace to them through today's session.

Engage the Scriptures

Unpack the meaning of Isaiah 40:1-11.

Solicit four volunteers to read Isaiah 40:1-2, 3-5, 6-8, 9-11.

Read or summarize the Bible Background for this Scripture to help participants understand the situation of the people of Judah and Jerusalem who first heard these hopeful words as captives in Babylon. They are being called to prepare for a new life.

Form several small groups. Encourage the participants to note the preparations the people are to make (verses 3-4) and the message they are to proclaim (verses 9-11). Prompt them to discuss these questions, which you will have written on a large sheet of paper:

1. What preparations do believers need to make to be prepared to welcome Christ?
2. What message are we as a congregation proclaiming to others by our words and our deeds about who God is and how God works?

Respond to two examples of hope.

Choose a volunteer to read the first paragraph of "Hope in the Holler" and ask: How is Bishop Woodie White's distinction between "leaving" and "going" helpful in providing hope for you, particularly in difficult situations?

Select another volunteer to read the second paragraph of "Hope in the Holler." Note that today's church has left its culturally privileged position of the 1950's and 1960's and is living into a new reality. Ask:

1. Why are some in the church holding on to the divine promise that God is with us as we move into this new way of being, whereas other believers desperately cling to the church they once knew?
2. What do you think Isaiah would have to say to both of these groups?

Interpret 2 Peter 3:8-15a.

Call on a volunteer to read 2 Peter 3:8-15a.

Discuss the following questions. Suggest that participants consult the Bible Background for this Scripture passage and "Delay Does Not Mean Denial" to delve further into the Scripture.

1. Why do you think the Scripture passage makes such a point of distinguishing between God's time and human time?
2. How does the passage explain the apparent delay of Christ's return?
3. 2 Peter 3:11 says that as believers wait they are to live "holy and godly lives." What do you think the phrase means?
4. What evidence suggests to you that believers are living "holy and godly lives" in this time between Christ's coming as a baby in Bethlehem and his coming again?
5. What evidence suggests to you that Christ's return is being delayed because the people of God are not living "holy and godly lives"?
6. What does the church need to do to help believers live so that God will hasten the day of Christ's return?

Roleplay a discussion based on 2 Peter 3:8-15a.

Encourage participants to silently read these verses from 2 Peter 3.

Read aloud the third paragraph of "Delay Does Not Mean Denial." Enlist two or more volunteers who will discuss the questions raised in this paragraph. At least one role player is to question whether the second coming will ever occur. At least one role player is to use ideas from Second Peter to explain that God has simply delayed this coming.

Delve into Mark 1:1-8.

Solicit one volunteer to read Mark 1:1-3 and another to read verses 4-8.

Discuss these questions. Add information from the Bible Background for this Scripture passage as appropriate.

1. How do you see the messenger prophesied in Isaiah as being fulfilled in John the Baptist?
2. What was the purpose of John's ministry?
3. How did people respond to him?
4. What distinctions did he make between himself and the One who was coming after him?

5. How did John help people to prepare for the ministry of the adult Jesus? (Recall that there is no Nativity story in the Gospel of Mark. Jesus is introduced as he is about to begin his ministry.)
6. In what ways are contemporary people being urged to prepare for the coming of Jesus? How are these ways similar to and different from the methods that John used?

Create a personal timeline.

Choose a volunteer to read Mark 1:1-8 in which the past of prophecy and the beginning of the good news of Jesus are linked together.

Dig deeper into the idea of the connection between different time periods by inviting another volunteer to read "Past, Present, and Future."

Distribute unlined paper and pencils. Ask participants to hold the paper sideways and draw a line across the center. At the far left, they are to write the year of their birth, and at the far right, 2017. Then they are to mark off segments along the line that represent a time span, perhaps five or ten years. Encourage them to recall events that had spiritual significance for them and locate them in the appropriate time span. These events may be directly connected to the church, such as baptism or confirmation. They may also be events that prompted them to draw closer to God or move further away, such as the loss of a loved one, the birth of a child, or losses due to a natural disaster.

Call participants together and ask:

1. What types of events ultimately caused you to grow in your spiritual life?
2. How did earlier events in your life prepare you for events that came later? In other words, what lessons did you learn that enabled you to move closer to God?

Close the Session

Commit to prepare spiritually for Christ's coming.

Distribute paper and pencils. Suggest that participants review the Scriptures they have studied today, thinking particularly about how they can prepare to welcome God anew into their lives by living in expectant hope. Challenge them to write two or three actions that they will take in the week ahead to be better prepared spiritually to celebrate the birth and coming again of Jesus Christ.

Offer a closing prayer.

Use these words from Ephesians 6:23-24 as a reminder of how believers can shine forth the love and peaceful presence of God during this Advent season: "May there be peace with the brothers and sisters as well as love with the faith that comes from God the Father and the Lord Jesus Christ. May grace be with all those who love our Lord Jesus Christ forever." Amen.

* Possible references consulted; footnotes refer to first editor's name or NIB or NISB: *Eerdmans Dictionary of the Bible,* edited by David Noel Freedman; *Feasting on the Word, Year B,* Volume 1, edited by David L. Bartlett and Barbara Brown Taylor; *Preaching Through the Christian Year, Year B,* edited by Fred B. Craddock, Carl R. Holladay, Gene M. Tucker; *The New Interpreter's Bible;* and *The New Interpreter's Study Bible.*

1. From *The United Methodist Book of Worship;* page 227 bottom A=Matthew 3:1-12; B=Mark 1:1-8; C=Luke 3:1-6.
2. From NISB; page 955, line 4.
3. See "Into Exile: From the Assyrian Conquest of Israel to the Fall of Babylon," by Mordechai Cogan, in *The Oxford History of the Biblical World,* edited by Michael D. Coogan (Oxford University Press, 1998); pages 264-266.
4. From NISB; page 955, "Second Isaiah."
5. From NISB; page 1008, footnote for 40:10-11.
6. From NIB, Volume XII; page 324, bottom.
7. From NISB; page 2189, third paragraph.
8. From NISB; page 2189, third paragraph.
9. From *Preaching Through the Christian Year, Year B,* edited by Fred B. Craddock, Carl R. Holladay, Gene M. Tucker; page 12, first paragraph.
10. From NIB, Volume VIII; page 533, right column top; NISB; page 1805, footnote for 1:7.

3. Anointed to Serve

BIBLE BACKGROUND*

On this third Sunday in Advent, the Gospel lesson again focuses on John the Baptist, though this week his witness to Jesus comes to the forefront. John made clear that he was not the Christ. Rather, he was the one to give testimony—"a voice crying out in the wilderness" (John 1:23)—to point all people to the "true light" (1:9) who was "coming into the world" (1:9). The good news announced by the anointed one to the lowly, oppressed, and poor in Isaiah 61 is the same news that Jesus will preach on behalf of the same audience (see Luke 4:18-19). Paul counseled the Thessalonian Christians, who were living (as we are) in the time between Jesus' first and second coming, to live expectantly for his return by constantly rejoicing, praying, and giving thanks.

Isaiah 61:1-4, 8-11

Christians studying this passage may think immediately of Jesus' reading of Isaiah 61:1-2 (and 58:6)[1] as he announced his mission in Luke 4:18-19. Earlier readers of Isaiah would have heard words about God anointing a figure for certain tasks. Biblical references to "anointed" ones include kings (1 Samuel 24:6), prophets (1 Kings 19:16), and priests (Exodus 40:15). This figure in Isaiah 61 may have been thought of as a prophet, priest, or king—or all three, as later generations viewed Jesus.

Although the figure is anointed for a variety of tasks, the work and those for whom the work is done share common traits. First, the work enables a reversal of fortune: for example, the poor hear good news; the brokenhearted are bound up; the captives are released; the prisoners are liberated; and those who mourn are comforted. Second, those whom the figure is anointed to help are all people who are in some way marginalized or deprived. References to "the year of the LORD's favor" (Isaiah 61:2) remind readers of the sabbatical year, which occurs every seven years, and also the Jubilee, which occurs every fifty years. These special events, described in detail in Leviticus 25, promised freedom for slaves, cancellation of debts, and a redistribution of property so that the family who originally owned it would not be left landless. Momentous change will occur: Even ruins will be rebuilt.

In Isaiah 61:1-4, the speaker is the Anointed One, but in verses 5-9 God is apparently the speaker. According to verse 8, God "loves justice" and will make "an enduring covenant." Once Israel has been restored to their proper relationship with God, all nations will recognize that God has blessed the people of Israel (verse 9).

A new, joyous relationship is described in verses 10-11 using two images: clothing and vegetation. The speaker referred to special clothes here: "clothes of victory," "a robe of righteousness," and wedding apparel of a bride and groom (verse 10). In verse 11 the growth of God's righteousness is compared to seeds sprouting forth.

1 Thessalonians 5:16-24

Written to the church in Thessalonica in about AD 50, this letter is generally agreed to be to be the oldest book of the New Testament.[2] The letter demonstrates the great affection Paul felt for this church he founded early during his second missionary journey. Although Paul could not revisit this church in Macedonia, he dispatched Timothy, who returned with a generally positive report. Yet 3:10 hints that something in their faith was "lacking" (NRSV), which is why Paul apparently wrote this letter.

In 1 Thessalonians 5:12-15, the apostle had given the church words of advice and encouragement as to how they were to live together as the people of God. In verses 16-24, which is our reading for this third Sunday in Advent, Paul addressed the inner spiritual life. In verses 16-18 we find three commands: rejoice, pray, and give thanks. These imperatives sound simple enough to obey, but note that none of these verbs is limited. Believers are to "rejoice *always*. Pray *continually*. Give thanks in *every situation* (emphasis added). Paul wanted believers to understand that rejoicing, praying, and offering thanks are not actions to be taken on an occasional basis but rather provide the framework for true worship of God in all facets of life.[3] Regardless of the circumstances—good or bad—these three commands are non-negotiable, not because Paul said so, but because they are the will of God (verse 18).

The three commands in verses 20-22 assure believers that they have a resource—the Holy Spirit—who will enable them to do what is good and avoid evil. But they must allow the Spirit to flow freely, so that they can listen to and evaluate the messages they hear.

In verses 23-24 Paul blessed the church, recapping themes he had raised throughout the letter: complete dedication to God (sanctification), God's call on their lives, and the second coming of Christ.[4]

John 1:6-8, 19-28

As was true in last week's reading from Mark 1, this week's Gospel lesson from John 1 again focuses on John the Baptist. Last week, we considered how John the Baptist pointed toward and prepared people for the coming of the Lord. This week, we hear John's testimony. Bearing witness to the Messiah was, after all, what he had been called and equipped to do.

In John 1:6-8, the writer of the Fourth Gospel sets forth his understanding of John's mission: to testify to the light so that "everyone would believe in the light" (verse 7). In the second part of today's reading from verses 19-28, John's words of witness are recorded. Readers can hear what he had to say about himself. The writer wanted to draw a sharp line between John, the forerunner of Jesus, and the Messiah himself. God sent John (verse 6; see also Luke 1:5-25, 57-80). But his purpose was to prepare people to follow Jesus by bearing witness to the Messiah. By inserting this description of John into the Prologue (verses 1-18) of this Gospel, the writer made clear that John himself was neither the Word, nor the life, nor the light.

When asked by the Jewish leadership to identify himself, John did so by stating who he was not. He was not the awaited Messiah (verse 20). He was not the prophet Elijah who was expected to precede the coming of the Messiah (verse 21). When pressed to provide an answer as to who sent him, John the Baptist quoted Isaiah 40:3 to indicate that he was "the voice crying out in the wilderness" (verse 23). Pushed further for more information about why he was baptizing, John said that he was unworthy to perform the work of a slave by untying the sandal straps of the One whom the religious leaders did not recognize. The next day John identified Jesus as the Lamb of God who had come to take away the sin of the world (verse 29).

SESSION PLAN

Open the Session

Hear and respond to words of joy.

Read Psalm 126:1-3 from the Common English Bible, which expresses the thanksgiving of the Israelite community for deliverance from exile in Babylon.

Ask: What causes you to feel joy in this season of Advent?

Offer an opening prayer.

Loving God, we come to you with joy on this third Sunday of Advent. Empower us by your Holy Spirit to serve you by using the gifts you have given us. In all that we say and do, let us testify to the good news that, through Jesus Christ, you have brought us out of the darkness and into the light of your blessed realm. Amen.

Engage the Scriptures

Study Isaiah 61:1-4, 8-11.

Choose two volunteers, one to read the prophet's words in verses 1-4 and 10-11 and another to read God's words in verses 8-9.

Form two groups, one to explore verses 1-4 and the other verses 8-11. Suggest that participants turn to the Bible Background and paragraphs four through seven of "Divine Exchanges" for help in answering these questions. Post these questions for verses 1-4:

1. For what purpose has the Lord anointed the prophet?
2. How do these purposes compare to Jesus' announcement of his mission in Luke 4:18-19?
3. How will the people's lives be different because of the work of the anointed one?

Post these questions for verses 8-11:

1. What do you learn about God?
2. What do you learn about divine intentions for God's people?
3. How does the prophet respond to what God has done?

Reassemble everyone and call on a spokesperson from each group to report their answers. Conclude by asking: Where do you hear good news in this passage that causes you to rejoice?

Contrast joy and happiness.

Ask: What is the difference between joy and happiness? (See the third paragraph of "Divine Exchanges.") List responses on a large sheet of paper on which you have drawn a line down the center and written "Joy" on the left side and "Happiness" on the right.

Point out that in today's Old Testament reading from Isaiah 61, the Israelites are no longer exiles in Babylon, but they are living in a corrupt society. Call on a volunteer to read Isaiah 61:1-4, 8-11 and then ask:

1. What reasons do God's people have to be joyful?
2. What similarities do you see between their situation and the situation of some people in twenty-first century America?
3. How might the exchanges that God promises bring joy to people today?

Consider joy and prayer as two sides of the same coin.

Choose a volunteer to read 1 Thessalonians 5:16-24.

Read this quotation from John Wesley, who "remarked that 'rejoice evermore' means that one is to live 'in uninterrupted happiness with God. Pray without ceasing—which is the fruit of always rejoicing in the Lord. In everything give thanks—which is the fruit of both the former. This is Christian perfection.'" (See "Living in the Light.")

Mull over these questions silently for the next two minutes:

1. What has been your experience in terms of how your prayer life affects your joy—and vice versa?
2. What changes do you need to make to move closer to perfection?

Invite volunteers to comment on their insights.

Describe how to live in the meantime.

Observe that as we journey through the season of Advent, we recognize that we are living in the time between Jesus' coming as God-in-the-flesh at Christmas and his return at some time in the future that only God knows.

Distribute paper and pencils. As a volunteer reads 1 Thessalonians 5:16-24, invite participants to list any action words (verbs) they hear.

Form small groups so that participants can discern what Paul's instructions may mean for them today. Suggest that each group look at the fourth and fifth paragraphs of "Living in the Light," which includes a quotation by John Wesley. Also suggest that they review the Bible Background for this Scripture passage.

Direct each group to choose one or two of the action words they listed and describe what taking that action might look like for them. How, for example, can believers who work all day, care for family members, and take care of the business of daily life "pray continually" (verse 17)? Encourage the groups to be as specific as possible in their descriptions of actions they can take.

Reconvene and hear from as many groups as time permits. Recommend that participants each take one action this week to live more faithfully in the meantime.

Investigate the mission of John the Baptist.

Choose one person to read John 1:6-8 and another to read verses 19-28.

Point out that John was being grilled by the priests and Levites, just as a witness might be questioned in a courtroom. Ask these questions, adding information from the Bible Background as appropriate.

1. Suppose you had been John. When the priests and Levites asked who you were, why did you answer by saying who you were not?
2. Suppose you had overheard the conversation between John and the religious leaders. What would you have asked him about the one who was to come after him?
3. As you think about your own life and mission, how would you answer the question, "who are you"? — follower of Christ
   — wife
   — engineer

Stage a talk show.

Select someone to read John 1:6-8, 19-28.

Invite four or five participants to stage a talk show for the rest of the participants. The group should designate one person as the talk show host, who will introduce the topic and keep the discussion on track. Group members will discuss what they heard John say and try to discern what they believe about John.

Include other participants by having the host call on people in the audience who want to ask questions.

Close the Session

Witness for Jesus.

Recall that we have considered how to live in the meantime—the time between Jesus' coming and his coming again. Living as one who is completely dedicated to Jesus includes rejoicing, constant prayer, and an attitude of gratitude in all situations. John taught us that faithful living also includes bearing witness to who Jesus is.

Encourage participants to reflect silently on their witness as to how Jesus has acted in their lives. Suggest that they think of a recent God-sighting, that is, something (large or small) that demonstrated for them that Jesus was at work in their lives.

Invite each person to partner with someone else and give this testimony. Recommend that participants be alert this week for opportunities to share with others the testimony they have just given.

Offer a closing prayer.

Use these words adapted from Henry Van Dyke's 1907 hymn "Joyful, Joyful, We Adore Thee:"[5] Joyful, joyful, we adore thee, God of glory, Lord of love. You are the wellspring of our joy of living. Teach us how to love each other so that we might dwell in your joy divine. Amen.

* Possible references consulted; footnotes refer to first editor's name or NIB or NISB: *Eerdmans Dictionary of the Bible*, edited by David Noel Freedman; *Feasting on the Word*, *Year B*, Volume 1, edited by David L. Bartlett and Barbara Brown Taylor; *Preaching Through the Christian Year, Year B*, edited by Fred B. Craddock, Carl R. Holladay, Gene M. Tucker; *The New Interpreter's Bible*; and *The New Interpreter's Study Bible*.

   1. From CEB; New Testament page 64, footnote k.
   2. From NISB; page 2115 (source of info for first paragraph).
   3. From NIB, Volume XI; page 733, bottom.
   4. From NISB; page 2121, footnote for 5:23-25.
   5. From *The United Methodist Hymnal;* 89 (Words from verses 1 and 3, which per page 907 are not copyright protected).

4. Humans Plan, God Laughs

BIBLE BACKGROUND*

On this fourth Sunday of Advent, we focus on Gabriel's announcement that a baby will be born to a young woman named Mary. Although God, not her fiancé Joseph, would be the father of this boy, Joseph played an important role in caring for Jesus and bringing him into the line of David (see Matthew 1:6, 16 and Luke 3:23, 31). Jesus was not Joseph's biological son, but he was still considered a descendant of his father's line. That point, which Luke stressed throughout his telling of the Nativity story, is crucial, for in 2 Samuel 7:16 God promised King David that his throne "will be established forever." Early Christians understood that Jesus was the One who fulfilled that promise. The proclamation of the good news of his birth marked the revealing of the God's "secret" about which the prophets had written (Romans 16:25-26).

2 Samuel 7:1-11, 16

Second Samuel 5 records the consolidation of Israel to the north and Judah to the south under the leadership of David. This warrior king fought to defeat enemies, particularly the Philistines who had captured the ark of the covenant. The return of this sacred chest and its placement in a tent is narrated in Chapter 6.

With his enemies now conquered and a "cedar palace" (verse 2) completed for his residence, David was able to enjoy the fruits of his labor—almost. David told Nathan that he wanted to build a house for the sacred chest. The prophet gave David permission. But that night God told Nathan that the chest had been housed in a tent since the days of the Exodus and that God had no interest in a permanent dwelling now.

God gave Nathan a message for David that turned on a Hebrew word that can be translated as "house," "dwelling," "palace," "temple," or "dynasty."[1] David was not to build a structure to house the sacred chest. Rather God would build a house—a dynasty—for David. This message begins in verse 8 with a reminder to David that he was tending sheep when God called him to tend the flock of Israel. Verse 9 makes clear that God had been constantly present with David. Moreover, God, not David, had "eliminated" Israel's enemies. God pledged to make David's name "great" and to ensure that he and the Israelites lived in peace, troubled no more by their enemies. In verse 11, God promised to establish a "house" (NRSV) or "dynasty" for David. Unlike most dynasties that only last for several generations, God said that David's "throne will be established forever" (verse 16).

Second Samuel 7 describes God's covenant with David. This covenant was crucial to the understanding the Israelites had of their relationship with God. They later assumed that because of this covenant no harm would come to Jerusalem or the Temple that David's son Solomon had built. When the Babylonians destroyed the Holy City in 586 BC and carted the people off to captivity, they wondered if God had abandoned them. David's throne was no longer occupied. Several centuries later, early Christians saw God's promise to David fulfilled when a child was born in David's city of Bethlehem and declared by an angel to be Christ the Lord (Luke 2:11).

Romans 16:25-27

These three verses close the Letter to the Romans with words of praise that begin and end with a focus on the glory of God, which is repeated three times in this brief doxology. Given the words in 15:6 about glorifying God "together with one voice," we can imagine that Paul was calling the entire church to lift their voices united in praise.

Just as the letter began with Paul wanting to visit the church at Rome "to pass along some spiritual gift to you so that you can be strengthened" (1:11), verse 25 ends the letter with a reference to God who could strengthen the believers with the good news of Jesus—an announcement that was written by the prophets long ago but had been kept secret. Paul made clear that this ancient mystery was now being made known to the Gentiles so that they might faithfully obey God. This announcement was well known even in the early preaching of the church. Believers were taught that the once secret mystery of God had been revealed through Jesus Christ.[2]

This doxology is especially appropriate on the fourth Sunday in Advent. The revelation announced here could only come about because Jesus had been born. God was with us to make known mysteries that existed throughout eternity but were just being made known at this point in human history.

Luke 1:26-38

Gabriel, an angel or messenger of the Lord, first appeared in Luke 1:11-20 to announce to Zechariah that he and his wife Elizabeth would have a son who would prepare people for the coming of the Messiah. Six months later, God sent Gabriel to announce to Mary that God favored her. The angel's appearance startled Mary, but after telling her not to fear, Gabriel went on to explain that she would give birth to a son who would be called "Son of the Most High." The son was to be named Jesus. This story is linked to the story of God's eternal covenant with David found in 2 Samuel 7. Gabriel said that God would give Mary's son "the throne of David his father"

(Luke 1:32). Furthermore, his kingdom would last forever (verse 33), just as God had promised David.

Mary was confused by this announcement, known as the Annunciation, because she had not had sexual relations. Gabriel explained that she would become pregnant by the power of the Holy Spirit. For God nothing is impossible. The angel pointed out that Mary's elderly relative Elizabeth, who had been barren during her childbearing years, was now pregnant. Hearing all of this, Mary responded as a faithful disciple—a servant of the Lord—giving permission for God to use her for divine purposes.

Luke told the story of the angel's announcement to Mary using a pattern that was familiar in the Jewish Scriptures.[3] (See Genesis 15–17, the announcement of Isaac's coming and his parents' response to it.) In these stories, an angel appears and a person reacts. The angel reassures the person and then announces that a child will be born, who is then named. A specific future is predicted for this child. The person to whom the angel is speaking raises an objection to which a final word of reassurance is given. At that point, the person accepts the angel's word.

The time to celebrate this birth is drawing very near. In the meantime, we can ponder this great gift that God sent into the world nearly two millennia ago. We can give thanks for Mary's example as an humble, obedient servant as we listen to God's call on our lives and respond with an exuberant "yes, Lord."

SESSION PLAN

Open the Session

Recall plans God vetoed.

Read the first paragraph of "Divine Vetoes" adding the Yiddish proverb, "Man plans, God laughs" as you read the first sentence.

Invite volunteers to recall plans they have made that God apparently vetoed. What had they wanted to do? What happened? In retrospect, were they able to see that God had a better plan for them? What effect did this experience have on their relationship with God?

Offer an opening prayer.

Gracious God, so often we have great plans for ourselves and seek your blessings on them, only to find that you have even better plans than we could ever imagine. As we continue our journey through Advent, open our eyes to those plans so that we might walk more closely with you. Amen.

Engage the Scriptures

Examine the two plans in 2 Samuel 7:1-11, 16.

Choose a volunteer to read 2 Samuel 7:1-11, 16 and then discuss these questions. Use information from the Bible Background as you find it helpful.

1. As you review verses 1-3, would you have said, as the prophet Nathan did, that David should go ahead with his plan? Why or why not?
2. What response does God make to Nathan in verses 4-7?
3. According to verses 8-11 and 16, what plans did God have for David?
4. This passage includes a play on a Hebrew word that can be translated as "house," "dwelling," "palace," "temple," or "dynasty." In what sense was David thinking of this word? In what sense is God using this word?
5. How does God's plan for David seem better than the plan that David had?

Recognize the impact of God's plans for David.

Select someone to read 2 Samuel 7:1-11, 16.

Delve into this Scripture by forming small teams to read the Bible Background and the final two paragraphs of "Divine Vetoes." Then discuss this question: How would the history of the world have been different if David had simply built a temple to house the ark of the covenant, rather than allowing God to build a dynasty through him?

Bring the teams together and ask:

1. What do the responses you heard within your groups suggest about the impact of even one decision that we might make?
2. Christians see the fulfillment of God's covenant with David through the birth of Jesus more than 900[4] years after David's death. What does that interval suggest to you about how God acts in human history?
3. David had to make a course correction. Are there any plans on the table in our congregation right now that may need to be reevaluated in light of God's plans for us? If so, how can we make that happen? How might we use the story of David to help others recognize that God may have other plans for us?

Analyze Romans 16:25-27.

Enlist three or four volunteers who have different Bible translations to read Romans 16:25-27. Encourage participants to listen for a range of meanings.

Discuss these questions. Use information from the Bible Background as you find it helpful.

1. What does this doxology say about God?
2. What do you understand to be the "secret" or "mystery" that had been hidden from view for ages?
3. Now that the good news about Jesus has been revealed, who will be able to benefit from that news?
4. How do these words prompt you to worship the Father and the Son?

Compose a doxology.

Lead participants in a unison reading of Romans 16:25-27. Encourage participants to review the section "Praise Your Way Through." Be sure to connect the ideas of praise and worship as related to the word *doxa*.

Distribute paper, pencils, and hymnals. Suggest that participants work individually or with a partner to locate doxologies in their hymnals that can serve as models for their own doxologies. (See, for example, "Doxology," page 951 of *The United Methodist Hymnal.*) Encourage participants to write a sentence or two of praise; setting that praise to music is optional. Call everyone together and invite volunteers to read their words of praise.

Overhear the Annunciation.

Select three volunteers to read the parts of a narrator, Gabriel, and Mary in Luke 1:26-38. Point out that this passage is referred to as the Annunciation, because the angel Gabriel is announcing God's message to Mary.

Raise these questions in response to the reading:

1. What role does Joseph play in Gabriel's announcement?
2. How does the pregnancy of Mary's relative Elizabeth enrich this story?
3. What do you learn about Jesus? What do you learn about Mary?
4. The text is not specific, but why might God have "favored" Mary?
5. How is Mary's role as the mother of Jesus scandalous? (See the first two paragraphs of the section "Scandal.")

Emulate the faithful obedience of Mary.

Invite participants to read silently the familiar story of Gabriel's announcement to Mary found in Luke 1:26-38.

Consider how Mary responds to the angel by choosing someone to read paragraphs three, four, and five of the section "Scandal."

Distribute unlined paper and pencils. Ask participants to fold the paper in half, from top to bottom. Next, ask them to draw a simple fish in each of the two sections of the paper. (Think of the fish used as an early Christian symbol and now often found on the back of a vehicle.) In the center of each fish, participants are to write something they felt God had called them to do. This task could be anything large or small, from taking care of an aging parent to chairing a committee to helping a neighbor. Have participants draw straight lines from the top of the fish upward. On each line, they should write reasons they tried to avoid this call. They are also to draw straight lines from the bottom of the fish downward and here write actions they took to answer the call.

Bring everyone together to discuss these questions:

1. What do your reasons for trying to avoid the call suggest about your willingness to obey and trust that God would equip you for the task?
2. What do your actions in answer to the call suggest about how you respond like Mary who said, "I am the Lord's servant. Let it be with me just as you have said" (verse 38)?
3. How might previous experiences when you have trusted God prepare and encourage you to respond when God calls in the future?

Close the Session

Lift words of praise.

Mary's Magnificat, found in Luke 1:46-55, is the song of praise today, rather than a psalm. Participants may read this passage in unison from their Bibles. Alternatively, if your hymnal includes these words as a responsive reading, use this format. (See, for example, page 199 of *The United Methodist Hymnal.*)

Recommend that participants say these words of praise each day this week as a sign of thanksgiving for God's gift of Jesus.

Offer a closing prayer.

Holy God, we glorify your name and rejoice that you have sent Jesus to be our Savior. His coming has transformed the world and changed our lives. We give thanks and praise for your grace, love, and mercy. Amen.

* Possible references consulted; footnotes refer to first editor's name or NIB or NISB: *Eerdmans Dictionary of the Bible*, edited by David Noel Freedman; *Feasting on the Word, Year B*, Volume 1, edited by David L. Bartlett and Barbara Brown Taylor; *Preaching Through the Christian Year, Year B*, edited by Fred B. Craddock, Carl R. Holladay, Gene M. Tucker; *The New Interpreter's Bible*; and *The New Interpreter's Study Bible*.

    1. From NIB, Volume II; page 1254, left column, second paragraph.

    2. From *Preaching Through the Christian Year, Year B*, edited by Fred B. Craddock, Carl R. Holladay, Gene M. Tucker; page 24.

    3. From *Preaching Through the Christian Year, Year B*, edited by Fred B. Craddock, Carl R. Holladay, Gene M. Tucker; page 25.

    4. From NISB; page 2295 dates for David 1000-960 BC

5. In Word and Song

BIBLE BACKGROUND*

We rejoice on this Christmas, which marks God's coming into the world in flesh. Isaiah looked ahead to a time of God's reign on earth and the good news of salvation that reign would bring. The readings from Hebrews 1 and John 1 help us to understand who it is who came, what it means for humanity that God's Son did come, and how this Word that dwells among us changes everything.

The Fourth Gospel reminds us that John the Baptist came on a mission from God as the first witness to testify to the light of the Son. Like John, we, too, are called to proclaim the good news of salvation and encourage others to open their hearts to believe in Jesus.

Isaiah 52:7-10

The prophet's words sound two themes: a call to praise God who reigns and the announcement of salvation. Today's passage opens by mentioning the messenger whose "feet" are described as "beautiful." Although this is a small detail, many people will recognize these words, which appear in Handel's *Messiah* (38 Air).[1] The music actually quotes Romans 10:15, where Paul made the word *messenger* plural ("those" in CEB) so as to refer to the early Christian missionaries. The focus, however, is not on the feet or even the messenger(s). Rather, the important point is the message. The messenger brings the good news of peace and salvation, which have come about because "God rules" (verse 7).

The sentinels who keep a lookout on the walls of the city of Jerusalem join the messenger in a song of praise, because "they see the LORD returning to Zion" (verse 8). In verse 9, even the places of Jerusalem that were destroyed and left in ruins at the time the people were hauled off into exile in Babylon are called to sing praise. The last part of verse 9 brings the reader full circle to the fulfillment of the promise in Isaiah 40:1-2, for the Lord has indeed "comforted" the people. Moreover, God has "redeemed Jerusalem." Consequently, the Lord is portrayed as victorious. The bared arm of the Lord (verse 10) refers to God's might and power in battle (see also 51:5, 9-11).[2] "All the nations" (verse 10) from one end of the earth to the other have witnessed God's victory.

Although this text specifically concerned the exiled Israelites who were to return home, these words are fitting for Christmas. God has come into the world in human form, and that is good news for all people. Our response to this good news, like that of the messenger and the sentinels of Isaiah's day, is to sing praise to the God of our salvation.

Hebrews 1:1-4 (5-12)

The majestic words of the unknown writer of Hebrews[3] begin in verse 1 with a reference to God speaking through the prophets. The time of prophetic revelation has ended, because now, "in these final days" (verse 2) God has spoken through a Son. The Son is described in verses 2-4.[4] He is God's heir of everything. The Son is also the One through whom God created the world. In the Son we see the brilliant light of God's glory. He is also "the imprint of God's being" (verse 3). The word *imprint* calls to mind a coin that looks exactly like the die from which it was cast. The Son is able to sustain and "maintain everything." He cleansed the people from their sins as a result of his death on the cross. When his purifying work was completed, he sat down at the right hand of God. Within these four verses the writer asserted not only the deity of the Son but also portrayed him as holding all three offices important in the Old Testament: prophet, priest and king.[5]

In verses 5-12, which are optional for today's lectionary reading, the writer used quotations from the Old Testament[6] to establish the superiority of the Son over the angels. Hebrews 1:5 uses a quotation from Psalm 2:7 to declare that the Messiah is God's Son. A second quotation in verse 5 is from 2 Samuel 7:14 where David's son is linked with the Son of God. Verse 6 includes a partial quotation from the Greek translation of the Old Testament, the *Septuagint,* of Deuteronomy 32:43 to show that Jesus is identified with the Lord God. Psalm 104:4, the quotation used in verse 7, compares the angels to changeable elements. In verses 8-9, Psalm 45:6-7 is summoned to show God the Father speaking to the Son, who is described in terms of a king. In verses 10-12, Psalm 102:25-27 refers to the Lord (and the Son) as the creator. Unlike creation itself, which will "pass away" (verse 11), the Son will "stay the same . . . [and] won't come to an end" (verse 12).

John 1:1-14

Unlike Matthew and Luke, which open with the story of Jesus' birth, John's narrative stretches across eternity to the beginning when "the Word was with God" (verse 1). Although the Nativity story is not told in the Fourth Gospel, John makes clear that "the Word became flesh and made his home among us" (verse 14). The eternal Word—*Logos* in Greek—entered history in human flesh.[7]

As John tells the story, the Word was not only "with God" but "was God" (verse 1). Like the creation story in Genesis 1 where God spoke and things came into being, in John "everything came into being through the Word" (verse 3). This Word was both life and light "for all people" (verse 4).

Verses 6-8, which we studied on the third Sunday of Advent, create an interlude in the eighteen verse Prologue to this Gospel. The camera moves from the Word to a man named John—not the Gospel writer but rather the one known as the Baptist. John was not the Messiah, but he was "sent from God" (verse 6) as a witness to that One so that through his testimony others would come to believe in Jesus, the light of the world.

This witness was necessary because as verse 10 points out, people did not recognize the light. Not even "his own people" welcomed him (verse 11). Many rejected him, but those who did welcome and believe in him became "God's children" (verse 12).

Verse 14 concludes today's reading with a confession that "we have seen his glory."[8] This glory reflects the Father's glory, for it is "full of grace and truth." John's description of the Word—the Son—reminds readers of the description of the Son as "the light of God's glory" as found in Hebrews 1:3.

Although this Gospel does not take us to a manger in Bethlehem to worship and adore a tiny baby, John does emphasize the incarnation of the Word that had been with God from the beginning.

SESSION PLAN

Open the Session

Celebrate the coming of the Lord.

Welcome participants. If possible, have on hand some light holiday refreshments that can be enjoyed throughout this session. If you plan to do this, you may want to contact group members during the week to see if they could bring some food or paper products.

Note that today's lectionary readings include Psalm 98. Verses 4-9 of this psalm are the basis for "Joy to the World." Choose either to read the psalm in unison or to distribute hymnals and sing the carol version by Isaac Watts (the *Hymnal*, 246).

Offer an opening prayer.

Gracious Lord, we sing praises for your salvation and give thanks that you have sent the Messiah to establish justice on the earth. Let our joy be so contagious that the whole world will know that you have come in the flesh to do new and wonderful things for us and for all creation. Amen.

Engage the Scriptures

Ponder the message of Isaiah 52:7-10.

Select a volunteer to read Isaiah 52:7-10. Post a large sheet of paper, and invite participants to ponder the news that the messenger proclaims. Ask these questions and record the answers on the paper:

1. What role has God played in bringing about the good news that the messenger proclaims?
2. What song or type of music do you hear as you read this description?
3. How does news originally intended for the Israelites to celebrate their restoration from exile seem appropriate as Christians celebrate the coming of the Messiah on Christmas?

Respond to Isaiah 52:7-10 with "happy feet."

Read Isaiah 52:7-10 as expressively as possible. Enlist a volunteer to read the first paragraph of the section "Thank God for the Message and the Messenger."

Talk briefly about liturgical dance. Ask: Have you ever seen this type of dance or danced this way yourself? How did it help you to enter into worship?

Select music prior to the session that is happy, energetic, and expresses the joy of Christmas. Arrange for a musician to play the selection for the group, or have recorded music and an appropriate player handy. "Good Christian Friends, Rejoice," "Angels We Have Heard on High," or "Go, Tell It on the Mountain" may be possibilities. Encourage participants to move to the music. If space is available, some may choose to dance. Others may prefer to stand and sway, whereas others may prefer to sit and move their arms and head.

Enter into Hebrews 1:1-4 (5-12).

Choose one reader for Hebrews 1:1-4 and, if you would like to include the optional verses, another reader for verses 5-12. Note that the first four verses describe God's ultimate messenger. The second portion shows how the Son is superior to the angels. Ask these questions:

1. What characteristics of the Son does the writer of Hebrews highlight?
2. What insights do you gain about the identity of Jesus from this passage?
3. Had you been the writer of Hebrews, are there other traits that you would have included? If so, what are they?

4. Why might the writer of Hebrews have included so many quotations from the Old Testament to make his points in verses 5-12?

Recall a Christmas tradition.

Select a volunteer to read the first two paragraphs of "When Mystery Meets the Mundane." Invite participants to tell about a Christmas tradition in their family that was, and perhaps still is, meaningful to them. Ask: How did this tradition help you to grow closer to Jesus or to more fully appreciate the impact he had on your life? Choose someone to read Hebrews 1:1-4 to summarize the person and work of God's Son.

See the light in John 1:1-14.

Observe that light and darkness are recurring images in the Gospel of John. Distribute small candles (which may be used for a Christmas Eve candlelight service). Invite all the participants to stand in a circle, if possible. Turn off the lights or, if you are meeting during the day, darken the room as much as possible. Ask one person to light his or her candle. Then, while this person holds the lit candle upright, the next person is to light another candle from the first one. Continue around the circle until everyone has a lit candle. While the candles are being lit, read John 1:1-14. You will probably want to have a small flashlight.

When all of the candles are lit, ask participants to look around the room and to "see" the light of Jesus in the face of everyone present. Read again verse 5: "The light shines in the darkness, and the darkness doesn't extinguish the light." After a few moments, invite participants to blow out their candles and return to their seats. Invite participants to contemplate these questions:

1. How is Jesus the light of the world for you?
2. How might you more fully walk in the light of Christ in your home, in your job, in your church, and in your social life this coming year?

Read verse 5 once again to conclude the meditation.

Poke holes in the darkness.

Choose three volunteers to read John 1:1-5, 6-8, 9-14. Ask participants to count the number of times they hear the word "light" (twelve times, CEB) as the passage is being read. Note that this repetition reveals the importance of the image of light.

Select one or more volunteers to read "Behold the Light." Talk with participants about the three groups of wavelengths and how this natural phenomenon seems to be related to the image that John uses for the Word.

Focus on the example of Robert Louis Stevenson describing the lamplighter as "a man poking holes in the darkness." Expand this image by reading Isaiah 9:2: "The people walking in darkness have seen a great light. On those living in a pitch-dark land, light has dawned." Ask:

1. Where are people walking in darkness in the world today?
2. How can you act as the hands of Jesus to "poke holes" in that darkness?
3. In what ways has this study helped you to "poke holes" in the dark places of your own life?
4. What will you do today to let the light of Christ shine through you so that others may see his light?

Close the Session

Review the Advent journey.

Invite participants to recall the first activity of our initial session when they were asked to think about new beginnings that they wanted to make. Distribute paper and pencils and ask participants to complete this sentence: As a result of this study, I have made the following new beginnings that have enabled me to walk more closely with Jesus...

Call on several volunteers to read their sentences. Challenge everyone to go forth from this session to continue to grow in the love and grace of Jesus Christ our Lord and to share the good news of his coming with others.

Offer a closing prayer.

Lord, we have heard the good news that in Jesus Christ you have brought us into the family of God. Empower us to be messengers who proclaim the good news of your peace and salvation; in Jesus' name. Amen.

* Possible references consulted; footnotes refer to first editor's name or NIB or NISB: *Eerdmans Dictionary of the Bible,* edited by David Noel Freedman; *Feasting on the Word, Year B,* Volume 1, edited by David L. Bartlett and Barbara Brown Taylor; *Preaching Through the Christian Year, Year B,* edited by Fred B. Craddock, Carl R. Holladay, Gene M. Tucker; *The New Interpreter's Bible;* and *The New Interpreter's Study Bible.*

    1. From NISB; page 1030 footnote for 52:7. See *http://www.worshipmap.com/lyrics /messiahtext.html,* (38) How beautiful are the feet. See Romans 10:15 (Isaiah 52:7).

    2. From NISB; page 1028, footnote for 51:5.

    3. From NISB; page 2151, third paragraph.

4. From NISB; page 2154, footnote for 1:1-4.

5. From NISB; page 2154, footnote for 1:1-4 (end).

6. From NISB; page 2154, footnotes for 1:5, 6, 7, 8-9, 10-12.

7. From NISB; page 1908, footnote for 1:14.

8. From NISB; page 1909, footnote for 1:14.